DOWN THE COLORADO

DOWN *the* COLORADO
Travels on a Western Waterway

BY JIM CARRIER

ROBERTS RINEHART, INC. PUBLISHERS

For Susan, colleague and companion on journeys yet to come

Also by Jim Carrier
Letters from Yellowstone
Summer of Fire

Contents

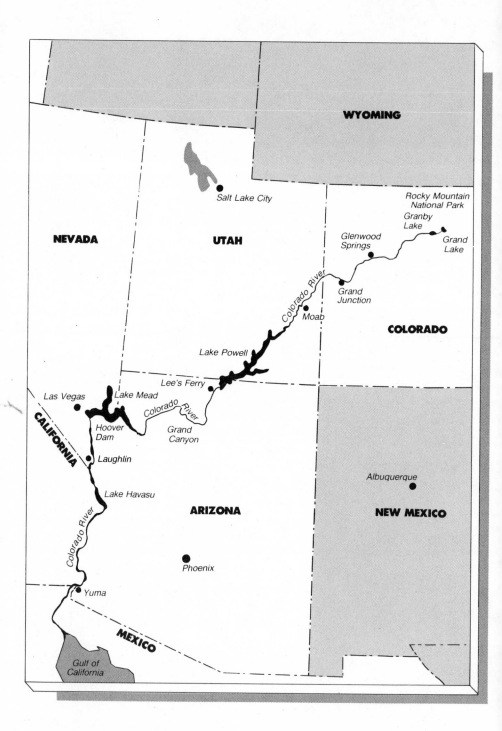

Acknowledgments

During my journey down the Colorado I carried a little notebook with names and numbers of people who provided background, history or facts about the river. They were segmented by the river section they knew best. Some I consulted before I left. Others I called frantically, and frequently, while on deadline from a phone booth somewhere, for a bit of information to add to a sentence. They were generous with their time. Without them, the trip would have been a mere travelogue.

They include: Dave Carlson, Jeris Danielson, David Walker, Dave Getches, John Rold, Dale Lashnits, Darrel Knuffke, Glen Kaye, Al Simonds, Dick Crysdale, Gary Schaefer, Linda Woodworth, Barry Wirth, Leon Hyatt, Al Jonez, Harvey Johnson, Chuck Troendle, Brian Werner, Bill and Fran Needham, John Holzwarth, Patience Cairns Kemp, Jean Naumann, Larry Parson, Sam Freeman, Mike Strang, Larry Pierce, Rollie Fischer, Orlyn Bell, Lee Harris, John Hamill, Jim Bennett, Bob Roth, Chuck Lundy, Butch Farabee, Ed Norton, Martin Litton, Georgie Clark, John Schenck, Dennis Underwood, George Wheeler, John Augustine, Don Brock, Steve Nelson and Frank Preciado.

Missing from that list, I realize, are countless people who helped me understand the river, who offered a cool drink, an anecdote and wisdom, and therefore a framework for the stories I found. Time has erased many of their names, but I am indebted.

I want to thank *The Denver Post* photographers and artists whose work is reproduced in this book. Graphics director Jerry Lundwell and assistant Ted Rogers arranged for the many maps and Artist Bruce Gaut drew most of them.

My editors on this project, Gay Cook, Tony Campbell and David Hall of *The Denver Post,* were visionary and supportive to the end. Moe Hickey, *The Denver Post* publisher, encouraged this book.

HEADWATERS
TO
GRAND JUNCTION

Sitting on a log bridge in Rocky Mountain National Park, the author takes notes as the river foams below. Photo by Jim Richardson

MAY 17

D raped like a blanket on the continental spine, a white, wet meadow set the stage.

It was broad as a wheat field and dotted with fir. Beneath the corn snow, the river formed.

I stood at La Poudre Pass, 10,186 feet, in the northwest corner of Rocky Mountain National Park, at the start of a journey down the Colorado River.

To the left was a mountain mass—bowls and gulches. To the right were the peaks of the Never Summer Range: Cumulus, Nimbus, Stratus, Richthofen. They were jagged and imposing.

Somewhere over there, at about 11,300 feet, was Lake of the Clouds, which I'd hoped with the heart of a poet I could claim as the birthplace of the Colorado.

But no such license was given; the lake was still frozen, and I probably would have died anyway in an avalanche of slush, trying to get there.

I was stuck with the prosaic truth: the Colorado, the great river of the West, began in a field of snow, nowhere in particular.

This, then, was where my journey would begin, too.

I planned to follow the Colorado River from start to finish, to travel by foot, raft, houseboat, car, plane and Lord knows what else.

For sticking close to the watercourse was a classic way to explore. To understand a river is to understand its region.

The Colorado was the West, the element that bound us together, and most divided us. I hoped to learn something about all that.

But here on the pass, on a warm spring day, that seemed a long way off. I still was looking for the river.

A bird's short toot sounded through the wind. The only sound of water came from a ditch behind me.

It was called the Grand Ditch, as if the name could make it pretty. It wasn't, just a gash in the hillside with a road beside, that ran across the breast of the Never Summers.

It sloped gently this way, to the north, carrying for 15 miles the spring runoff into a reservoir, then into the Cache La Poudre River, for farms and homes in Fort Collins.

Occasionally the wind carried the sound of a backhoe digging snow from the ditch so water could flow backward across the Continental Divide.

Even before the river had a running start, its waters were taken.

I struck out, in search of another beginning, picking my way past the deepest snow. I carried snowshoes in my pack.

Within 200 yards, I heard water again as the meadow dipped and the valley of the Little Yellowstone took shape. The walls steepened. Stones, then rocks, then boulders filled the ravine.

The valley was a "U" wrapped by the divide, which ran south with the river in its loins. In the distance, I could see the Gore Range.

I inched along the side, my boots slipping on the mud. Snow lay in the bottom, but water ran beneath. I could hear its muted murmur.

Around a bend, the creek appeared in a hole in the snow. It giggled like a child, high and persistent after a game of hide and seek.

I bent for a drink and it slapped me cold. I dropped my map in the water.

I emptied my bottle of city water, filled it from the stream and stood up. Flecks of debris floated in the bottle. It tasted good.

I had found the river, and was surprised to feel less joy than melancholy. It had been, after all, a difficult birth.

Yet the running water tugged at me, and I walked on.

MAY 18

The making of a river is a wondrous thing to watch.

Like veins on a leaf, running to the main stem, streams of water rush to the Colorado.

If you walk along the gathering river, as photographer Jim Richardson and I did at the headwaters in Rocky Mountain National Park, water surrounds, and drowns out all else.

Most of it emerges from springs, which run after snow melts into the ground. They can be seeps, just wet spots on the forest floor, or gushers, emerging from holes a foot across.

As they run on the surface, the water picks up debris—and color. We saw gray, red and chocolate.

We even walked in water up to our waists—or so it seemed, so laden with moisture was the snow still piled in the park.

It drenched our pants as we postholed through. The snow-shoes were useless, sinking to the ground. I put on gloves, because my hands could touch the snow with each step, and I was stumbling.

It was the worst time to travel in the mountains, but the best time to watch a river form.

It is snow that makes a river in Colorado, not spring rains or summer thunderstorms. That is why measuring the snowpack is so important.

The depth of snow in the Rockies on April 1 is all a farmer needs to know to plan his irrigation. What is on the ground then is all he can count on.

This year snow was down 25 percent in the mountains that feed the Colorado. In the park, in the valley we walked, it was even less. Despite the gush of spring, despite our wet legs, this would be a drier year.

At 9,500 feet, the valley broadened and the river slowed. It was now about 10 feet across, a foot deep, and slightly gray with silt.

As it reached the site of Lulu City, the old mining town, the Colorado met its first dam: willow and mud, thrown up by beavers.

We stopped to eat on a grassy bank dried by the sun. We lay back and snoozed.

A little more than 100 years ago, the beaver had to give up their waterworks after someone found flecks of gold in a pan here. A city sprang up, more of hope than substance.

Within four years, the beavers took it back. All that remains are cabin foundations and a log grizzly trap, half hidden by trees.

For the next few miles, the river runs undisturbed, growing slowly. It is home to trout, muskrats, even otter which have been brought back to the park by man.

But this is not wilderness. For many years this stretch of the river was homesteaded.

There were famous dude ranches, like the Never Summer Ranch, where Sophia Holzwarth held forth, cooking with water dipped from a stream that ran past her kitchen. Her husband, John, had come to Colorado after driving cattle with Charlie Goodnight in Texas. He liked to drink with his buddies, but "Sophie"—known as "Mama"—rebelled at feeding them. She started charging, and thus began the guest operation.

The river was center to it all. The dudes fished in it, their kids played in it, their horses ate hay flooded by it.

In the 1970s, the Nature Conservancy bought the ranch and sold it to the park, which tore most of the ranch down, all but Mama's old cabins.

If you walk the mile from Trail Ridge Road, and peek behind the old cook shack, you can still see the little pool in the stream where Mama dipped water for her guests.

MAY 23

As the ice moved away from shore, a mirror appeared at the edge of the lake, reflecting the mountains that surround it.

The water was still and dark, just wide enough for a hint of snow-covered Mount Craig and a sliver of Shadow Mountain's forested hulk. Leaning close, I could see the sun sparkling.

To my eye there is nothing prettier than a mountain lake nestled by snow peaks, doubling the image in the calm water. Grand Lake is such a place.

For many years, the lake was advertised as the headwaters of the Colorado River. That was a simple notion, back when the lake's outlet created a streambed.

Today, that streambed is gone, buried beneath a reservoir.

But Grand Lake remains, a dowager from a gentler time when society came to escape the heat.

The town of Grand Lake sits on the north shore, a strip of tourist glare surrounded by a colony of cabins, clinging to what little land lies between the shore and the mountains.

Old Victorian cottages, each with a boathouse, encircle the lake, their slabwood shutters pulled tight against the winter. Old families and old money still haunt these cottages.

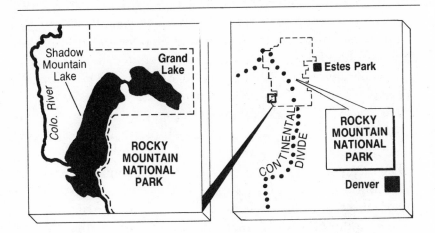

Accompanied by their servants, they came with their families over Berthoud Pass from Denver, Kansas, Texas. Frank Hall of Hallmark came from Missouri and built a house reachable only by boat. It still is in his family.

In the town, there was a ballroom and big bands and moonshine. Mac Ruske, who grew up there, earned money picking up pint whiskey bottles beneath the elevated ballroom floor.

There also was the yacht club, built of unpretentious slabwood but very private.

Then, as now, a cottage on the lake meant membership in the club.

It is the world's highest yacht club, at 8,437 feet, listed with Lloyd's Register of Shipping, and dating to 1902.

The setting, on a lake one mile by two, makes for tricky sailing. As Mary Cairns described in her history of Grand Lake: "A sudden squall will sometimes capsize a boat but all mountain yachtsmen have taken their spills with the grace of true sportsmen."

The annual regatta revolves around the Lipton Cup, presented in 1812 by Sir Thomas Lipton, an English tea scion and yachtsman.

Tall silver, with gargoyles and gewgaws and bands at the bottom for inscribing the names of winners, no cup before or since — not even the America's Cup, which eluded Sir Thomas five times — is coveted more by a group of yachtsmen.

When members gather each August for the blessing of the fleet, they stand below Lipton's charter, mounted on the mantel, and his photograph aboard his yacht "Shamrock." He is in full sail and his famous mustache is flowing in the wind.

They also pass a glass case preserving a menu from that wonderful evening so long ago when Lipton came to Denver at the invitation of the club.

The menu displays Lipton's shamrock (his parents were Irish), faint ribbons of the club's colors, a script in French on velvety paper, and a stain of something elegant in the corner.

The Lipton Cup goes home each summer with the winner

of the regatta. It is displayed proudly on mantels unless the winner isn't home. Then, said Ruske, the cup is hidden in the laundry, closets, even the shower.

"I hid it under the bed," said Ruske, a past commodore who once won the cup. "It's irreplaceable."

MAY 24

To a kid in the country, a stream is a magic playmate in spring. It never tires, it endures our games, and it carries a sense of timeless joy, which is what childhood is all about.

I used to pile rocks to make dams so water would rise to my knees and I could "swim."

I dug tiny trenches from the streamside, fascinated at how water ran in them. I'd shovel frantically to stay ahead of the flood. Then I'd dig a tiny pond to float my sticks.

The first diversion of the Colorado River is not so different: a cut in the bank of the river, carrying water to someone's playground.

The ditch, the first of thousands on the river, is just outside Rocky Mountain National Park. Here the river winds through the flatland across gravel beds, good habitat for native cutthroat trout.

The cut, maybe 2 feet across, is lined with vertical pine poles to stabilize the bank. The water flows a half-mile from the river along the high side of a hay meadow and spills through the grass — flood irrigation.

The meadow is "lawn" for vacation homes built along the river here. It also feeds Ken Bruton's horses.

"I need the hay," drawled Bruton, a Texan who boards horses and sells land for summer homes. The water also runs into a pond in front of those homes.

The big log house Bruton built for himself is strewn with the pelts of beavers that tried to dam the irrigation ditch.

A mile or two down the river, to the west of Grand Lake, someone has piled rocks in the river to form a pool, just as I once did. Here the water collects against a concrete wall and two big rusted metal gates — the headgate for the Red Top Ditch, which runs 13 miles to five ranches west of the river.

The water from this ditch floods enough meadow to raise 4,000 tons of hay, much of it sold to Front Range horse owners.

But even this ditch is child's play compared to the diversion ahead: the Colorado Big Thompson Project.

The river tumbles out of a hillside and into Shadow Mountain Lake, a reservoir south of Grand Lake. Shadow is connected by a short stretch of river to Granby Lake, the heart of a massive plumbing system that sends water east of the Continental Divide.

Water from the Colorado and numerous other streams collects in Granby. A 13-story pump house, sunk into the lake's edge, pushes the water upstream, through Shadow Mountain, up the old streambed, into Grand Lake.

There the Adams Tunnel, a pipe 9 feet across, drains water 13 miles beneath Rocky Mountain National Park to Estes Park.

Tumbling down the east face of the Rockies, the water creates a perpetual-motion machine; the water turns five turbines that generate the power to pump the water that turns the turbines.

The water runs to Boulder, Fort Collins and other cities for homes and businesses, and on to 700,000 acres of farmland.

This water irrigates 30 percent of Colorado's agricultural output, with an annual value of $235 million — $75 million more than the Big Thompson Project cost in 1937.

On the western side of the Continental Divide, where the water is collected, agriculture has been displaced by tourism. Along the chain of lakes, cottages and condominiums cover the pastures. The lakeshore at Granby is one marina after another.

I stopped for a beer at the Gang Plank, a bar and marina housed in an imitation boat the size of Noah's Ark. Joe Murray, one of the owners, was looking out the window at the receding ice. Buoys lay forlornly on the mud flats.

This time of year, Granby Lake is empty, drained of its water, ready for the runoff.

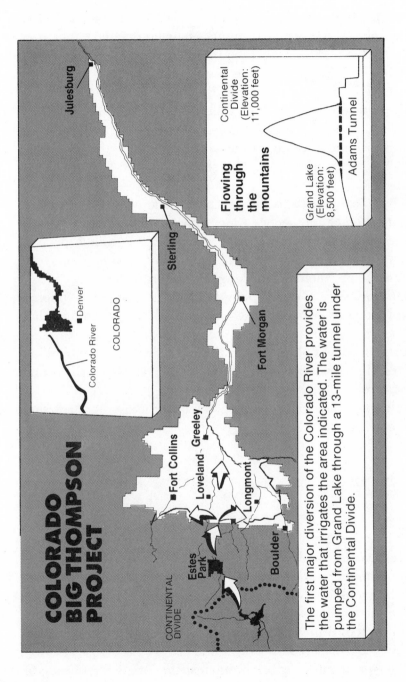

COLORADO BIG THOMPSON PROJECT

CONTINENTAL DIVIDE

Estes Park

Fort Collins

Loveland Greeley

Longmont

Boulder

Julesburg

Sterling

Fort Morgan

Colorado River

■Denver

COLORADO

Flowing through the mountains

Continental Divide (Elevation: 11,000 feet)

Grand Lake (Elevation: 8,500 feet)

Adams Tunnel

The first major diversion of the Colorado River provides the water that irrigates the area indicated. The water is pumped from Grand Lake through a 13-mile tunnel under the Continental Divide.

By July, when the boats return, the buoys will be afloat again. It's tough, said Murray, running a marina on a lake that goes up and down 18 feet in three months.

The river, in all of this, is lost.

The Big Thompson Project diverts to the Front Range 90 percent of the water that has collected at this point in the river system.

It is just one of 22 diversions in the state that takes Colorado River water from its vast watershed across the Western Slope of the Rockies.

There are pipes and ditches, siphons and tunnels draining about 600,000 acre-feet of water a year. That would fill more than two Dillon Lakes, enough water for 2.5 million people.

That is 4 percent of the total Colorado flow and 20 percent of the river's water that belongs to Colorado.

Driving below Granby Dam, I failed to recognize the mighty Colorado. It was a gentle stream again. The law requires that just enough water be released to keep fish alive.

In a meadow by the stream I found Calvin Nobles working a fire. He wore boots and carried a shovel. He was burning weeds from a ditch.

In another week he would open a gate for another diversion of Colorado River water.

MAY 26

For all its popularity, the Colorado River is a loner on its journey to the sea. It wanders off by itself, away from ranch houses, away from the roads that mimic its grade. Only the cottonwoods and tamarisk give its path away.

For the most part it shies away from cities, which is my practice, too. But when I came to the first one on the river, Hot Sulphur Springs, I stopped.

The spring sun was bright against the long white façade of the Riverside Hotel.

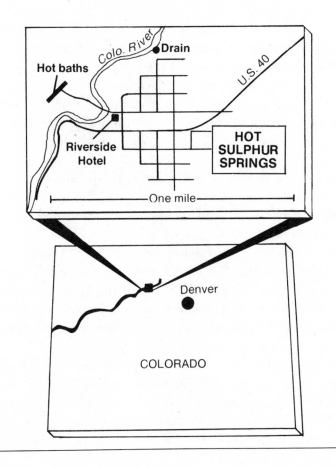

There were no other cars in front. Abraham Rodriguez, the owner, was inside the foyer, arranging geraniums. His curly head showed through the glass.

He showed me to a room overlooking the river.

A sink was in the corner, there was a writing table, and a simple iron bed with a colored quilt nearly filled the room. The bath was down the hall.

"I don't get the Bavarian plastic crowd," he said, handing me a key to the front door. "This land has kinda withered on the vine. Before I-70 was built, this used to be a main drag to Salt Lake."

Rodriguez moved to Hot Sulphur Springs from Boulder. His roots lie in Spanish Harlem, and like most New Yorkers he is excitable about many things. Like the new cable-TV channel the town chose — Nashville over Arts and Entertainment.

"I tell this town by the catalogs in the post office," he said. "You have to be lovers of horses and guns and Dallas. The other day I saw a Bonwit Teller catalog. Who would get Bonwit Teller here?"

There was a time when Hot Sulphur Springs was a major Rocky Mountain resort, when the railroad dropped passengers from the East to relax and recuperate in the hot springs that ran from the rock above the river.

Zane Grey wrote in a cabin nearby. John Wesley Powell reconnoitered in Hot Sulphur Springs and practiced running rapids before his historic trip through the Grand Canyon.

The city always has drunk from the river. Today, a little way up from the hotel, a pipe sticks out in midstream, the first section of a system that sucks water from the Colorado. The water is used by 450 people, passes through sewage-treatment lagoons, then returns to the river 200 yards downstream from the intake.

That water is the town's biggest revenue source, bringing in $70,000 a year. The man in charge of the treatment system is a proud, stocky gun dealer named John Kinder. He showed me through.

"See, you're standing on what ya call a clear well. Nothing but a big holding tank's all it is, really. This here tells us how much water we've got in the tank."

He showed me digital readouts of pH and turbidity and bragged how few chemicals Hot Sulphur Springs adds to its water. "You go to Kremmling, they use three or four different things we don't use."

He waved his arms at the pipes: "Chlorine shoots up here, over here, up here and jets back through here. The alum attracts particles and makes a sinker out of them."

I thanked him and walked across the only bridge in town to the hot springs.

Whatever the glory days, the baths were a bit run down. Windows were broken out of the old pool building. Sulphur stains were everywhere. Although nothing could live in the hot, acidic water, I wasn't so sure when I stepped into the clammy, dimly lit room where the water swirled in a pitted pool.

The truth is, owners Bob and Jimmie Ivie didn't have their hearts in the business anymore. They would like to sell and move to Arizona.

"There was a couple here this month," said Bob. "They asked what the profit was. I said there is no profit. And they said so why should we invest in it. And I said beats me. We've lost the ambition to go ahead and develop it."

Jimmie, a biologist who inherited the resort from her parents, said business was good only in the summer. Many customers were regulars.

"They come here, rest their bodies, and walk back and forth to town. All that helps the baths limber them up. But as far as it being a cure, we don't promote it."

Once they checked the possibility of making the springs a private club, like a successful spa in the San Luis Valley.

"They sell memberships and they run around naked," said Bob. He showed me a directory of hot springs all over the West. Many were illustrated with nudes.

He giggled and pointed to Jimmie.

"She's a little old-fashioned. We'd rather not get into that stuff. We'd rather sell it and let somebody else worry about it."

MAY 29

There couldn't be a more "western"-looking river bottom than the ranch country near Troublesome.

Tall cottonwoods nearly hide the river, their leaves a blush of spring. Green fields spread away from either side, filled with cows and their babies.

On the ridge above, sagebrush grows. Above that, snow still shows on the peaks of the Eagles Nest Wilderness.

Driving by, it is picture perfect. But in some respects, the ranch scene is a façade.

Just over that sagebrush-covered ridge, for example, on the shore of the Williams Fork Reservoir, is a healthy-looking, productive spread that's not worth much as a ranch.

Jim Taussig owns it. He was out burning weeds from irrigation ditches when I went to talk to him. I followed the smoke across barbed wire, past a grazing bull, and flagged him down.

More than 20 years ago, Jim's dad, burdened with estate taxes from the death of two brothers, sold his water to the Denver Water Board. Denver agreed to let the family irrigate 40 more years. That time is up in 2003.

Jim, now in his 60s, has tried to sell the land, but no one wants a ranch without water.

If he still had the water to sell, Jim said he'd do as his father did. "The way ranching is right now, I don't enjoy it. The banks own the cattle and the machinery and the Federal Land Bank owns the land. It's times like this, when ranchers are tight, that they're ready to deal."

A neighbor, Carl Breeze, just sold his ranch to the Denver Water Board for $1.4 million. Denver didn't buy it for the land but for a small, key water right below the Williams Fork dam.

Neighbors were shocked. Carl had fought Denver's water grab—that is what it is considered on the Western Slope—for years.

"If I'd been younger, I'd never sold my ranch," said Carl, who is 86. "It was old man age."

It seemed like everywhere I went in Middle Park, people told of yet another ranch sold to Denver. The water board owns more than 10,000 acres in Grand County. Each sale removes the land from the county tax rolls, but the bigger concern is loss of water.

Even though water can be bought and sold like land in Colorado, a line I heard often is: "They're stealing our water."

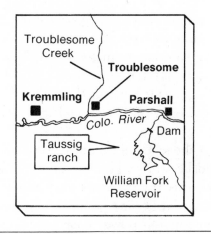

As I walked through ranches along the river, full of life this time of year, I tried to imagine them as dry and sagebrush-covered. I thought of the infamous Owens Valley, the pretty mountain farm country that Los Angeles dried up by building an aqueduct to it and buying all the water.

Similar scenarios are painted in Grand County. Growth in Winter Park and Fraser, prime recreation areas, is being strangled by lack of water. And Denver's thirst is not quenched.

Denver gets a third of its water from the Colorado and most of the rest from the Platte River. Water for future growth would come from the Colorado. The Two Forks Project, for example, would double Denver's draw on the Colorado.

Another Denver proposal would pump water in a pipeline from Green Mountain Reservoir, along the Blue River, to Dillon Reservoir, a key Denver storage facility. Enough water would be released by Denver to maintain the Blue River as a prime trout stream.

Oddly enough, fishing will prevent Denver or anyone else from drying up the Colorado, because minimum stream flows protect aquatic habitat on the river.

A group of ranchers near Troublesome who are fighting Denver use fish, not cows, as their main argument. Most of them lease their property to private fishing clubs for $2,000 to $10,000 per mile of river frontage.

"Up until 10 years ago, ranchers could give a hoot about tourists," said Steve Herter, who manages Elktrout Lodge, an expensive guiding business across the river from Troublesome. "Now they recognize that the tourist dollars can keep their operations afloat."

The Colorado above Troublesome Creek is Gold Medal trout water and could be world class, he said.

"As it is now, this river doesn't have many friends. These ranchers by themselves aren't going to affect minimum flows. They don't have enough power base."

After talking to Steve I got out my fly rod and whipped some water. The river was clear, cold and about 50 feet wide, bubbling over small rocks. A great place to fish, but they were safe from me.

I gave up and stopped at the Bar Lazy J dude ranch, which sits among the cottonwoods on the river bottom just below the town of Parshall.

"Denver can't afford to dry this river up," said Chuck Broady, whose dude ranch caters to tourists. "This is a real playground for Denver."

MAY 31

Finally, I got on the water!

I stepped into a rubber raft below Kremmling, bundled up against the spray. It was cool and somewhat overcast, a little early for rafting. I hoped the raft would stay upright and dry.

This stretch of river is the first place on the Colorado River suitable for floating.

Above here, the river cuts through upper Gore Canyon, churning at the granite restraint. The white water, made all the more dangerous by huge chunks of rock blasted to build the railroad, is run only by experts in kayaks and crash helmets.

Below the canyon, the water spreads out in a little valley, site of the Pumphouse, a popular boat ramp for rafters, run by the Bureau of Land Management.

The river, I was told, is a gentle glide with a few spots of white water to State Bridge, 14 miles away, or 60 all the way to Dotsero. That stretch was a good place for a beginner like me.

When I told friends I was following the Colorado River, they assumed I would get in a raft and float like a piece of driftwood, I suppose, 1,450 miles. At four miles an hour, I theoretically could reach the Pacific in 15 days, not counting some hellacious portages.

But I'd have a good case of what they call raft rump, and I suspect I'd have left most readers somewhere upstream. Rafting is best done in small doses.

I caught my first ride with BLM men who issue permits, set up picnic and toilet areas, and try to keep peace between landowners and rafters.

Each summer, 40,000 people float between the Pumphouse and State Bridge, mostly on weekends.

We buckled on life jackets, pushed off into the brown current, and immediately returned to shore. They had forgotten a bail bucket, which sounded ominous. Underway again, Dave Cooper worked easily to row us into midstream.

I immediately began peppering him with questions: statistics, history, the names of birds. There is something about a float trip that opens your mind to natural history; a good boatman comes prepared.

The pace is slow enough to see things you'd miss whizzing by in a car. You hear things you'd never hear.

A dipper bobbed in the water, a king snake ate a squealing chipmunk, swallows swarmed in a fresh hatch of caddis flies.

We stopped at a little hot springs in the rocks, known only to rafters.

The river kept building as small creeks tumbled in — Little Blacktail on the right, Sheephorn on the left.

We splashed through a few rapids in lower Gore Canyon. Dave did nicely; I stayed dry.

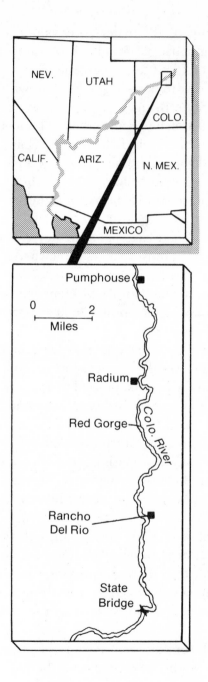

It's impossible, sitting there with nothing between you and the river but a thin, rubber skin, not to connect with the natural world. Even things I could care less about—some old ruins of a cabin—prompted ruminations about its occupants as we drifted by.

I was like a little kid. I've never been so curious—or hungry.

When we stopped to eat at Radium, I asked where the name came from. Poor Dave, he shook his head.

Then a new bird flew over.

"There are three kinds of birds," he said. "Big brown birds, little brown birds and non-brown birds."

I laughed every time I saw a bird that afternoon. Floating on down, we were quieter, lost in our private thoughts.

There had been plans to dam the river in this stretch, but the idea was killed by the rafting community. Another threat, they say, is Denver's future water needs, which rafters fear would eliminate rafting here.

Rafters can show millions of dollars in benefits to river communities. It's also a nice, clean, sport, provided beer cans are picked up. It uses water and lets it go.

We entered Red Gorge, as beautiful as its name. Signs on the riverbank warned us to be quiet.

In Colorado, the landowner on a river owns everything but the water—the land beneath, the air above—and can shut off access. The owner along here threatened to, unless rowdy weekend rafters kept it down.

We splashed through another set of rapids. By now the sun was out, and I enjoyed the spray.

Then we hit flat water, where the oarman works the hardest. We pulled out at Rancho Del Rio, a private rafting company just above State Bridge.

The river was slow chocolate here. As we drove away, it just kept rolling along.

JUNE 2

The grand entrance to Sybil and Charlie Settlemeyer's humble abode is from the river.

You can dock your boat on their lawn of alfalfa, push your way through the geese, open some of the 27 gates Charlie has welded over the years, and climb to the old square-log cabin, half buried in the ground, the outside covered with farm tools hanging on pegs.

Their 90-acre homestead lies in a bend of the Colorado River north of Bond. The Rio Grande Railroad bridges the river to the north and south of the cabin, providing the only dry access to their land.

That's how I got there, by walking across the north bridge.

Sybil was off fishing by herself, where the river runs quiet. She sat in an orange director's chair in a blue knit suit, apron and brown hat. Her face was lined with years, and she talked, as Charlie did, with the speed of someone no longer in a hurry.

"We've got three burros, two horses. We got rid of our cows. We have geese, turkeys, chickens. We irrigate alfalfa, we have a big garden. We may be old but we manage all that.

"Oh my. . . ."

She grabbed her pole, which was propped in a forked stick.

"Sucker, I can tell ya." She reeled the line from the muddy water. "I told you it was a sucker. If they don't break the water, they're suckers."

Every morning Sybil walks across the south bridge and drives to work at the local landfill, collecting fees. Charlie, who is 75 and arthritic, stays home and putters.

I found Charlie at the river's edge, pouring gasoline into a Briggs and Stratton 5-horsepower engine. He pulled the starter rope a couple of times, it caught and water surged through a pump onto a tiny alfalfa plot near the river.

"A person can lose his water right if he don't use it," he said. "That's why I keep mine up. I need it."

He walked slowly past the old house, built in 1894, and puddled water into his dry garden.

"You ever see a Pikes Peak squash? They're about that big around. For pie, or custard, they're sweet. I raise tomatoes here you can't believe, and corn and squash and beans, cabbage and broccoli. My wife is quite a canner."

Behind him sat a huge pile of sheet-metal, fenders, wheels, tools and vehicles, strewn everywhere. Charlie caught me looking at it.

"When I came here it looked like a disaster area," he said. "Well, it kinda looks like a junk yard. But I've got anything you want. If you can find it."

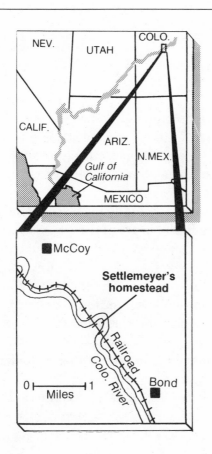

The Settlemeyers bought the old place in 1969 and closed up their Denver tire shop to settle here.

They made early peace with the river and railroad. If the river flooded, they hauled their pump higher and rebuilt the bank.

Charlie built good fences so that cows no longer wandered onto the track. "They haven't killed an animal since I've been here," he said. When one of the bridges caught fire, he turned in the alarm.

The railroad lets them use the bridges to bring stuff in, vehicles, machinery, more scrap metal. There it stays.

"That's as far as it goes," said Charlie. "This is the end of the line."

JUNE 4

An old man in the club car played a raunchy tune. Brakes squealed an accompaniment. There was rhythm everywhere: the swaying cars, a guitar, the railroad, the river.

The Rio Grande and the Colorado have shared the same trail so long the two seem entwined, travelers together through spectacular country.

The river cuts a gentle grade for both, through canyons and ranchland, through the heart of the Rockies. Watching it pass aboard the California Zephyr is one of life's gentle pleasures.

The day I rode, every seat in the lounge car was swiveled to the river. Next to me was an elderly couple from Chicago, on their way to see a great-grandson in Montrose. On the other side was a Louisville family, headed to Glenwood Springs for a weekend soak.

As the train moved along, a conductor told stories over the public address system.

On some runs, conductor Craig Billings spins a yarn about Thelma Addlefinger, a river runner who races the train to Glenwood. Despite his vivid narration, no passenger has yet seen her.

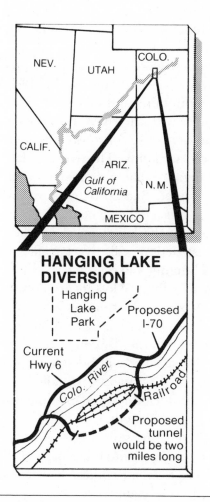

And it was too early in the season for rafters to give Amtrak passengers their cherished Colorado Salute, a moon en masse.

We had to settle, instead, for scenery unmatched: red rock and sagebrush, a turkey buzzard hunting, apple blossoms by the river, winter white on a distant peak. A dozen times, the scene went black as the train disappeared into tunnels.

"You see things every trip you've never noticed before," said Frank Danicic, a senior conductor. More than once train crews have saved hunters' and rafters' lives by diving off the track into the water.

The line was first built by David Moffat to haul coal and ice from Craig to Denver.

It was on the Glenwood Canyon run that a General Motors engineer conceived the Vistadome, the bubble glass rail car that opened up the mountains and canyons.

As we descended with the river, I was struck by the change in seasons. Gone were wisps of snow. The foliage was lush and dark. A dogwood blazed pink. The river had fallen nearly a mile.

We passed Hanging Lake, a short steep walk up a side gulch to a high pristine pool. Backed by creamy waterfalls and surrounded by ferns, it is a delicate glade in a rough rock canyon.

Someday hikers to the lake won't hear the interstate traffic below. New construction will divert traffic through a 2-mile tunnel around Hanging Lake.

By then, Amtrak will have lost its pre-eminent vista of Glenwood Canyon. A bike path, running alongside the new Interstate 70 at the river's edge, will allow hikers and riders to use this canyon for the first time. By connecting with the old U.S. 6 and existing paths, a biker will be able to peddle from Glenwood Springs to the Continental Divide.

In places the path is cantilevered over the water. Whitewater rafts will pass at arm's length.

Rocks have been cut and stained to imitate the natural canyon wall. Willows are being planted in cracks in the riprap, which was carefully placed to create eddies. The landscaping is a commendable effort by the state.

But I can't help wondering how the river will respond, squeezed even more between the new road and the rail line.

Engineers designed the bike path to be flooded without washing away. But the river will decide.

JUNE 7

The power of the river finds a voice in ancient instruments. Inside a concert hall of old yellow metal, they spin and roar: ceaselessly, monotonously, as antique dials with Edison script keep time.

Around the clock Chuck McClain and his men conduct the alchemy of turning water into electricity. From the copper bars at the shed's west end, the power climbs the walls of Glenwood Canyon from the Public Service Co. Shoshone plant and disappears into the grid.

By modern standards, it is a puny generator — 15 megawatts an hour. The PSC's Cherokee plant in north Denver produces 400.

But it works, as it has since 1909, with the precision of fine machinery kept tuned: General Electric, Allis Chalmers, the names still stand behind the polished plaques.

The plant is simple. Colorado River water, diverted by a dam through a tunnel, tumbles through tubes into two turbines. Their shafts spin openly in the plant, at 400 revolutions per minute, moving coils of wire past magnets, creating alternating current.

The water is straight from the river, filled with sand and sticks. Sometimes the sticks will wrap in the turbine. When that happens, McClain's men, working in a glassed case to protect their ears, can feel the vibrations.

By the time the Colorado River reaches the Shoshone plant, the river is an enormous force, measured as all rivers are in cubic feet per second.

A flow of just one cubic foot per second would fill a city bus in an hour. The water in the bus would weigh 110 tons.

Where the Colorado leaves Granby Dam, high in the mountains, the river's flow is 75 cubic feet per second. That is the equivalent of 75 buses filled with 8,000 tons of water.

Tributaries add to the flow. When I was there, the Williams Fork added 116 cubic feet per second; the Blue River added

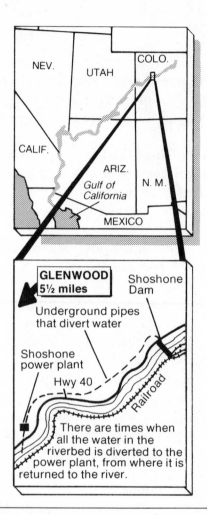

300; the Eagle was 1,450. By the time the river reached Glenwood Canyon, it was running at 4,080 cubic feet per second.

That's the equivalent of 4,080 buses filled with half a million tons of water, moving at 30 miles an hour. And the buses just keep coming, in a continuous stream.

At peak capacity, the Shoshone plant uses 1,400 cubic feet per second to run its turbines.

The Western Slope counts on that much water running through the plant and on to other users.

Shoshone power plant manager Chuck McClain stands at the diversion dam above Glenwood Springs. Photo by Karl Gehring

Last year, however, the Denver Water Board and Public Service agreed that in dry years Denver could divert more water at the upper end and pay Public Service for the lost power at Shoshone. Each cubic foot per second that is taken away reduces the plant's output by 11,000 watts.

The day McClain showed me around, the river was running well above the plant's capacity, spilling generously over the diversion dam, setting up a ferocious whitewater spray.

"You're looking at approximately 3,000 cubic feet per second," McClain yelled as he stood on the dam. "If you can imagine 23,000." That's what the river reached in May 1984, during a record runoff. Twenty-three thousand buses roaring down the canyon at 174 miles an hour.

"I hope I never see it again," said McClain.

Before I left the plant, McClain showed me the gates that screen debris from the river before it heads into the tunnel.

Logs, dead deer, dead sheep are routine. Three human bodies

were pulled out over the years. A can of ashes, too—the cremated remains of a Minnesota man.

"We pulled the can out, brought it down here, and tossed it back in the river," said McClain. "Sent him on his way."

JUNE 11

I spent a few days in Glenwood Springs, living in a hotel that overlooked the river.

The railroad depot was below, and several times a day a train whistled by. Twice each day the big Amtrak cars pulled in, dropped off people with dry bathing suits and picked up others carrying wet suits in plastic bags.

From the depot, I could hear the shrieks of children playing in the hot springs across the river.

I stayed awhile because I liked Glenwood. For a city crammed in a canyon, it's easy to get around. I walked most places.

For a tourist town, it's surprisingly genuine. Age, I suppose is one reason. The city, with old sandstone hotels and some good restaurants and shops, is comfortably commercial.

The hot springs pool is clean and attractive. I went late one afternoon, just as the air was cooling, and the water was a delight.

I swam some laps, then sat and watched. Kids cavorted, athletes splashed, couples promenaded in chest-high water.

I don't know what the medicinal value is, but people have come for generations to soak in the natural hot water. Buffalo Bill Cody even traveled from Denver for the cure. He died five days later.

There is no geologic connection between the hot springs and the river. But Glenwood Springs is central to the politics of the Colorado.

The river's water court, the water engineer, the conservation district and some old-time water law firms are based here.

The Western Slope's water battles have been waged from Glenwood. Plans for the Colorado's future are being made here.

There is a deep parochialism in this canyon, stemming, I guess, from the river itself. Water attracts us, maybe involuntarily, primordially, as a reptile ancestor was drawn to an ancient swamp.

Before it goes, something inside whispers, "use the water. Grab it before it runs away." Greed only compounds this basic instinct.

I received a letter complaining that I didn't understand the river system. Denver, the reader wrote, does not get water from the Colorado. It gets it from the Blue River or the Fraser.

To simplicity, I plead guilty. I have chosen to confine my travels to the mainstem of the river, to consider the entire watershed "the Colorado."

Fact is, most of the story of this river is in the tributaries. That's where the water is taken, that's where the dams will be built — scores of them, I dare say.

Although the era of federal megadams may be past, hundreds of smaller dams have been proposed on practically every stream. Catch that water, the dam builders say, before it gets away.

Many existing dams in the Colorado watershed were built to compensate for the diversion of high mountain water to the Front Range. The dams catch excess spring runoff and release it later downstream. The Williams Fork is such a dam. So is Green Mountain.

Dam building today is more a political struggle than an engineering feat. Each dam means a fight, and if built, an ongoing struggle for use of the water.

Nowhere is this better illustrated than up the Roaring Fork Valley from Glenwood Springs.

In the 1960s, as part of a diversion of the Frying Pan river to the Arkansas River, Ruedi Reservoir was built north of Aspen.

Built in a classic damsite, in a narrow red-rock canyon, Ruedi creates a deep and beautiful lake, ringed by national forest.

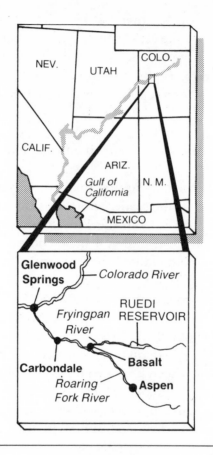

When it was built, the water was set aside for the usual reasons: agriculture, industrial and municipal use. There were plans to build irrigation canals down the Roaring Fork valley.

Times changed, though. The farmland filled with vacation homes and condominiums. The oil shale industry collapsed. Water collected in the reservoir.

Aspen added a power plant, producing 40 percent of the city's electricity. Fishermen discovered the world class trout habitat below the dam.

Campgrounds were built on the lake. The Aspen Yacht Club floated a dock. Wind surfers found a favorite beach.

When the Bureau of Reclamation recently announced the sale of the water in the reservoir, as originally intended, all hell broke loose.

I thought of the kids in the pool in Glenwood. In Colorado, there's nothing like a good water fight.

JUNE 12

The Grand Valley opened before me, a wide and rich land that marks the end of the Rocky Mountains and the beginning of the Colorado plateau.

This once was sand dune and sea country. The lines of the landscape run horizontally, layers of sediment exposed by the river, which runs broad and slow.

The names of the towns are arresting to a wanderer — Silt, Rifle, Parachute. I drove into each one, only to find ordinary villages with good streets, sidewalks and new city halls. Beneath the streets ran new water and sewer lines. Oil shale money had been there.

Silt got its name from the river. Over the years there have been proposals to change it to something fancier.

"A fella came through here with a lot of big ideas and said we ought to change our name," said local historian Betty Savage. "He said we could attract more people. I think it's going to take more than that."

I asked her what kind of names. She giggled and said it was too embarrassing. "C'mon," I said.

"Well, with a gun museum and Rifle next door, somebody came up with Gunsmoke."

Near the top of the banded shale that rises behind each city is the dark brown line of the Mahogany Ledge. In that band, in places 40 feet thick, 1.8 trillion barrels of oil are locked in rock.

To get it out with existing technology, we will need 4.5 trillon barrels of water. That's what they mean on the Western Slope when they talk about "future needs."

USING WATER TO PRODUCE OIL

Water is a key ingredient in producing synthetic fuel. Roughly 2½ barrels of water are used to produce one barrel of oil.

FIRST, FIRE . . .

Rocks containing shale oil are heated to temperatures reaching 900°. A substance called kerogen cooks off and is used to make synthetic crude.

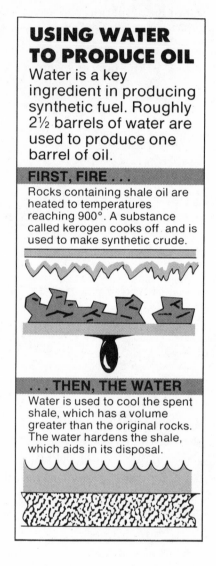

. . . THEN, THE WATER

Water is used to cool the spent shale, which has a volume greater than the original rocks. The water hardens the shale, which aids in its disposal.

"Nobody's going without now, but if we ever need it, we may not have it," said Jack Terry, ringing up sales at the Silt Market.

"Denver's stealing our water," said Mary O'Dell, a customer. She laughted and pointed to Jack. "We're both from Denver. We used to water big lawns." (About half of Denver's water goes to water lawns.)

"Don't you have lawns here now?" I asked.

"Yes," she said. "But they're smaller."

The sense that the Colorado is drying up is common on the Western Slope. Throughout this river trip I have looked for evidence. It seems to be an old wive's tale.

The fact is, the majority of the water in the Colorado leaves the state unused.

California and Arizona have a legal right to two-thirds of that water. Colorado has a right to one-third.

But because Colorado lacks dams to hold the spring runoff or industry or agriculture to use it, at least a third of the state's rightful share of water, between 700,000 and 1 million acre feet, flows across the border.

That's a lot of water. Seven hundred thousand acre feet would supply a city twice as large as Denver.

Having said that, however, I realize that water is finite. If oil shale were to boom again, if the Front Range grows again, if agriculture were to expand, then Colorado's unused water could disappear.

Oil companies own 500,000 acre feet of water in the river and on the ranches they purchased. But no one expects that water to be used soon.

Union Oil's plant in Parachute is producing 4,000 barrels of oil a day, using about 11,000 barrels of water in cooling towers and the disposal of the residue ash. It's the only oil shale plant in the United States and still is in a test stage.

Last month, the townspeople celebrated the fifth anniversary of Black Sunday, when Exxon pulled out and the oil shale industry collapsed.

Today the major industry is retirement. The proposed

7-Eleven is a retirement center. The cemetary at Battlement Mesa, across the river from Parachute, is filling up.

"I don't see a resurgence in oil shale," said Bobbie Wambolt, who grew up with it.

She remembers small plants in the 1920s. Her father shipped pieces of mahogany shale to Chicago for experiments in the 1930s.

He sold his ranch to Union Oil in the 1950s and leased it back for taxes. Bobbie's late husband, Marvin, worked for years for the oil companies and carved bookends from the beautiful shale.

Now she rents a modular home from Exxon for $225 a month, including utilities and yard care.

"They have turned it into a beautiful place," she said. The fine ash of the oil shale process has settled, and that suits her.

"I washed it out of clothes for 30 years."

JUNE 14

George Anderson didn't look like an executioner. An open face with glasses, a gold tooth behind an easy grin. Friendly, soft-spoken. Dressed in work pants, work shoes, driving a pickup truck.

But each year George lowers a device that resembles a guillotine. He screws down people's irrigation gates, shutting off their water.

George is a water commissioner, a state water cop who controls water in Roan Creek. He has been doing the job 50 years. Before that he drove for his grandfather, who was commissioner before him.

In the incredibly complex world of water rights, George makes it look simple.

From a dusty, cracked briefcase he pulled five sheets of paper. On them, listed 1 to 177, were the water rights in his district.

George Anderson, a water commissioner, controls gates and destinies on Roan Creek near Debeque. Photo by Karl Gehring

No. 1 was the oldest, dating back to 1883, No. 177 the newest. They varied in amounts of water. The date was the key. The water court in Glenwood Springs assigned the number based on when the original owner began putting water to beneficial use.

That court, one of seven in the state, assigned numbers to 17,000 water rights on the Colorado and its tributaries.

"It's priority," said George, simply. "The whole district is adjudicated."

George stuffed the briefcase back in a closet and we headed out in his pickup. He carried all the numbers in his head.

"This here's the 147 AA ditch," he said. "That's reservation ditch, with 21, 60 and 84." The ditch carries water with three different priorities.

The priorities are important; they determine who will get water and who will not. By July, after the spring runoff, George is shutting gates.

The ditch with No. 1 priority gets its water, no matter what. If it means shutting off No. 177, George goes out in his truck and does it, attaching a tag to the gate, declaring his action.

No. 2 also will get water, maybe at the expense of numbers 176 and 175.

In most years, after mid-July, George is out daily on the 70 ditches in his district, adjusting flows. In his shirt pocket is a flume gauge for figuring water flow.

If No. 10 is entitled to 5 cubic feet per second, he may have to close No. 174 with its 2 cubic feet and No. 173 with its 3 cubic feet.

When a high priority right is short of water, the owner makes a "call" on the creek, calling for his water. George lowers some gates until the call is met.

"I go up and measure, and if I'm short the adjudicated right I have to come up the creek to make up the difference.

"I'd rather do anything than go tell a guy I've got to shut his water off," George said. "If you don't have water up here, you don't have nothing."

Even a good water right is useless if there's not enough water. A number of years ago, a Texan moved into Roan Creek.

"I used to turn enough water in to fill his cistern and irrigate his garden," said George. "His priority was 63. It was dry years. He eventually sold out and went back to Texas. That's all the water he had in eight years."

In the drought of 1977, the ditches of former Rep. Mike Strang of Carbondale went dry, despite his senior rights on Cattle Creek.

He was forced to get a drought loan. Combined with a failed television investment, his financial woes became an issue in his loss last November to Ben Nighthorse Campbell.

On the main stem of the Colorado River, the senior rights are the Public Service Co. Shoshone power plant in Glenwood

Canyon and what is called the Cameo call for irrigation near Palisade. Both date to the turn of the century.

All upstream users are subject to shutoffs, according to priority, to meet those calls.

Exceptions can be made, however, if there is a reservoir. For example, Denver releases water from its Williams Fork Reservoir to meet downstream calls while it drains creeks higher up.

On Roan Creek, Texaco and Conoco will do something similar, pumping water from the Colorado to meet senior rights on the creek. The companies will then divert normal creek flows upstream for their oil shale operations. It's worth millions to ensure oil plants a reliable source of water, free from downstream calls.

Under Colorado water law, oil companies and old boy ranchers are treated the same, according to their priorities. It's just that the big boys can better afford litigation in the nation's only state water court.

That's why half the water lawyers in the country live in Colorado.

JUNE 16

A peacock was crowing in the bush-choked yard. A rabbit was playing with a cat by the steps. "Lonesome Dove" was propped open on a chair in the shade. The last petals of yellow roses, still fragrant, were scattered on the ground.

I was standing before a big blue farmhouse near the Colorado River in Clifton. The owners had offered to put me up.

I jumped at the chance. A home-cooked meal, a refrigerator raid at midnight, a sofa to stretch on, a home away from home.

I didn't expect to find a place as interesting as this, though, or the beginning of a story.

The screen door opened and Claudia Rector stuck out a hand. She was cheery, brunette and a walking encyclopedia about the river next door.

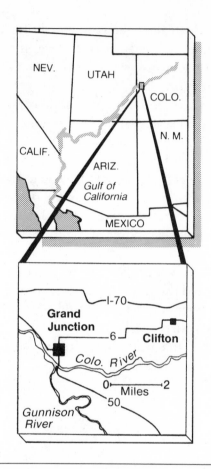

Claudia, a biologist, and her husband Walter, a computer consultant, live on the edge of a wetland formed by the Colorado. When the river floods, a swamp is created in an old gravel pit area, and all manner of bushes and plant life grow.

It looked pretty wild to me; to Claudia it was paradise.

"Right now, I can hear maybe 35 types of birds," she said. "There's a sora rail, only found in marshes. There's a black-crowned night heron. They need the trees to roost in, the marsh to feed."

The Rectors and other birders have documented hundreds of species of wildlife in the riparian zone along the river. Their work shows that the river is a valuable habitat. Even old gravel pits make wonderful waterfowl and fish areas.

"Oh look!" She touched my arm. "A wood duck. I never come here without finding a surprise."

We stepped under a cottonwood. "Unfortunately, a popular use of this river bottom is trash," she said, pointing to a car seat.

The Rectors, I learned, are part of a movement in the Grand Junction area to turn the river into a scenic wildlife and recreation mecca. Their home stands near the head of what someday could be a greenway through Grand Junction.

But there is a lot of work ahead. The car seat is symbolic of more serious problems.

One of the nation's biggest uranium tailing piles is on the bank not far from downtown. Just downstream from that, junkyards spill autos into the river; some of the cars are said to be radioactive.

Throughout the valley, gravel pits have torn up the river. The confluence of the Gunnison and the Colorado rivers, for which the city was named, is lost in an industrial zone.

"You can't get to the river, you can't see it. It's a disaster area when you get to it," said Karl Metzner, the city's planning director. "It's pretty typical of cities all across the country. The rivers always tended to be the industrial areas, the dumping grounds."

What surprised me, however, is that Grand Junction only now is contemplating a riverfront revival.

People have talked about creating a Colorado River park here for years. The drawings gathered dust on a shelf. It has taken a federal project to move the tailings to renew interest.

Although lacking a coordinated approach, a variety of people and groups are embracing the greenbelt idea.

The Lions Club hopes to buy a chunk of land now used as a junkyard and make a park. The Audubon Society has opened a bike path, built by volunteers, on the west side of town.

The city wants to redevelop the industrial zone, to move the junkyards and attract new businesses.

Grand Junction's neglected riverside is slated for cleanup at the confluence of the Colorado and Gunnison rivers. Photo by Karl Gehring

Sculptor Dave Davis, who runs the local arts center, has even offered to weld a giant brontosaurus from car bodies at the Fifth Street Bridge, the south entrance to Grand Junction. At least, he joked, the critter would distract tourists long enough to get them past the junk and into the city.

Davis, jolly, blond and bearded, used to roam the desert country looking for scrap metal for his sculptures. He took me to a hill overlooking the confluence of the rivers, the highway and railroad bridges and the junkyards beyond. "I think everyone in the community thinks it's an eyesore," he said. "But if you look right here."

He pointed to the trees and shrubs growing on the banks between the bridges. Several birds flew in and out. "This," Davis said, "is more valuable than we thought it was."

"The Colorado is a diamond in the rough," added Gary

Fergusen, the city's development chief. "Good waterfront property is hard to find. We have it. We just haven't decided what to do with it."

JUNE 20

It isn't every day that you come across a man, scantily dressed and sweating, bearing a timber and crosspiece on his shoulders, walking a cactus-lined path in the wilderness.

"What is this," a startled hiker asked the man. "Some kind of Easter re-enactment?"

"No," said the man, who turned out to be Hank Schoch, a ranger at the Colorado National Monument. "But it made me feel like Charlton Heston."

The story, which Schoch retold on another after-hours hike up the same path, says a lot about the monument. A small place, full of serendipity, where a ranger will work on his own time, building a trail.

Schoch hopes others will follow in his footsteps to see his "cross" — a sign that marks the trail. At least that would get people out of their cars, to learn something about this little-known park.

Carved in stone beside the river, the Colorado National Monument is a microcosm of the plateau country that stretches west and south with the Colorado River running through it.

An uplift cut by erosion, one canyon after another, with spectacular monoliths and carved red walls, the park climbs 1,400 feet from the valley floor. People who happen upon it feel as though they've discovered it.

"It's pretty small," said Schoch, one of 14 employees. "You can come out and have the feeling you have the whole place to yourself."

About 800,000 people visit each year, more than half of them local people going to work on the paved road or just out for a picnic. The monument is, in many ways, a city park for Grand Junction.

Ranger Hank Schock built a trail after hours at the Colorado National Monument near Grand Junction. Photo by Karl Gehring

Schoch pedals his bike up the steep grade to work. "I never see anybody else. I never even see footsteps," he said. "Yet if I need a quart of milk I can go two miles in the other direction and be in City Market."

The monument was created by a hermit considered crazy by many, John Otto, who dug and blasted the first paths into the rock in the early 1900s. But the park has suffered an identity crisis because of its name.

"Colorado" just doesn't have the ring of Canyonlands or Arches, of which it is a nice preview. "This is a little more intimate, a little easier to digest," said Schoch. "You can see lots of structures and formations in a short time."

But the name, he said, is a nuisance. "It doesn't evoke an image of anything. It would be nicer if it had a catchy name."

"Rimrock" was once proposed. The Coors bike race, which runs through the park, calls that leg "Tour of the Moon."

People come to the park to climb, walk, study geology or camp. You can camp anywhere away from the road or trails, or in the 80-unit campground, which is rarely full.

"Here we encourage people to get off by themselves. You can't get lost here," said Schoch.

From a sandstone ledge he swept his arm to the north and east. From almost anywhere in the park you can see Grand Junction, and all canyons lead to the river.

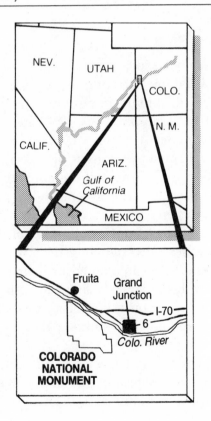

"You can get stranded, and obviously if you walk off a cliff you can get hurt," he said. "It's a neat place to seek your own values, walk your own path."

Schoch, who has been at the monument 10 years, started building his path along an old water line to enable visitors to reach the historic Black Ridge Trail, high on the plateau, that Indians and pioneers used.

The average visit to the park is about two hours, mostly from the seat of a car. Less than 2 percent of the visitors ever venture beyond 50 yards of the road.

That's why Schoch built the trail. "There is an awful lot here," he said, "if they get out of their car."

JUNE 21

Through the hash of a radio transmission I could hear the faint tink-tink, like a hammer striking metal under water.

I twisted the small antenna in my hand and the sound faded, disappeared, then came back. As we headed upstream near Clifton, it grew louder.

Near an eddy formed by a tongue of gravel, the signal grew strong. Doug Osmund turned off the outboard. Through the green earphones I clearly heard it. Bleep-bleep. A sound from the belly of an endangered fish.

In the Colorado River from Grand Junction down, fish most of us have never seen are signaling their whereabouts to researchers through radios implanted in their abdomens.

They are fish with strange-sounding names: humpback chubs, Colorado squawfish, razorback suckers. Once common to the river, they are endangered species, their numbers in the hundreds.

Unlike other endangered species, the grizzly, the wolf, the eagle, there is no popular support for endangered fish. Only a mother could love a humpback.

A bugged, blind razorback sucker is lowered into the river by biologic technician John Anderson. Photo by Karl Gehring

They are considered by many as trash fish and were once poisoned by the state.

Even researchers for the U.S. Fish and Wildlife Service, charged with "saving" the endangered fish, labor in ignominy while they study how to do that.

The fish are a powerful reminder of what we have done to the Colorado River in a century of civilizing the West.

Where once the river ran unchecked, flooding then ebbing, muddy and warm, it now is dammed and diverted. Water released from the dams runs cold and clean.

Fish that had adapted to the old river were lost in the new. They were slim fish with muscular humps and strange bony growths. The bonytail chub was the most common fish in the river in 1800. Today it may be gone. Only two have been found in a century.

A squawfish bumped a boat of Maj. John Wesley Powell when he was exploring the Colorado; it was thought to be a rock or a whale. Squawfish grew to five feet and 100 pounds. Today they are still sizable, 15 to 20 pounds and more than 30 inches long—not bad for a toothless minnow.

But they are confined now to a few sections of the Colorado and the Green rivers. The fish we tracked in the boat was a squawfish.

Dams are the greatest threat to endangered fish because they block the river and change the temperature and clarity of the water. Low water also is a threat to the squawfish. In the Grand Junction area, recovery efforts are aimed at buying or forcing the release of enough water to keep the squawfish afloat.

There are times, late in summer, when nearly all the Colorado is diverted above Grand Junction to water fruit trees, grapes and alfalfa in the Grand Valley. That is when squawfish spawn.

"People wonder why we should care, when they're already in bad shape," said Lynn Kaeding, who heads the federal endangered-fish study team in Grand Junction. "I can only assume that if you maintain conditions for the squawfish, you will also maintain conditions for a riparian ecosystem."

Kaeding showed me a pond where young squawfish are being raised. But he would rather not stock the river. "If we need to use a hatchery, something has gone wrong" with the natural habitat, Kaeding said.

But a hatchery could be part of a political solution to allow continued diversion of the river. Endangered species are capable of stopping development, as the snail darter did in Tennessee. In Colorado, however, agencies and developers are working to provide enough water and streambed habitat to maintain some fish.

Near the hatchery pond, Kaeding led the way to the riverside, where a razorback sucker was being implanted with a radio.

The fish had been caught before—a red tag was snapped to its dorsal fin. Both eyes were clouded and the fish, about five pounds, had not grown much since the last catch.

Chuck McAda first put the fish into a galvanized tub of anesthetic, then turned it on its back on a board. With a scalpel, he slit the yellow flesh.

"She's female," he said. A small trickle of blood ran from the cut.

With forceps, he held the battery-powered radio, encased in plastic and measuring about one by three inches, then slid it into the incision. With shaking hands, he sutured the incision and put the fish into a tub of river water to recover.

"We getting a signal?" he asked, as one of the technicians put on the headset. It was a strong wick-wick.

When the fish began to move, she was released in the river. It was an eerie feeling.

Only three razorbacks have been radioed in the years of study. No young have been caught. "If we have 200 or 300 in the Colorado, I'd be surprised," said McAda.

"This thing is a dinosaur," said Kaeding. "It really is. When these die, that's the end of them."

I can't say that I felt love for that particular fish, struggling to stay alive and now dragging a radio.

But there was definitely a feeling of sorrow as the fish, blind and bugged, was lowered into the murky waters of the Colorado and slowly disappeared.

GRAND VALLEY
TO
LAKE POWELL

JUNE 25

It was raining hard as the Jeep crept across the wet, rickety bridge and into the orchard. Peach trees, planted to the edge of the brimming canal, glistened and dripped, their new fruits just visible as hard green nuts. Beneath the trees, water ran in furrows.

I pulled up at a little house among the trees and dashed to the door. The man who answered had the look of someone fresh from a shower.

"I just came in wet," laughed Curtis Talley. "I was out checking water."

He had been out in the rain—irrigating. He assured me that didn't happen often in Grand Valley.

"This was a desert when people first came here," he said. "They used to haul water in barrels with a wagon and team, and pool the water around each peach tree."

Today, fruit growers like Talley dip water from canals, and run it through pipes, and then into furrows among the trees.

"Trees need deep moisture," he said. "It can rain, but it doesn't wet it like irrigation does."

One hundred years after men were encouraged to settle this desert with plentiful, cheap water from the Colorado River, the Grand Valley is still an oasis, a green sweep of terraced, trained trees that startles the traveler.

The river still keeps back the desert. Water is diverted upstream at Cameo by an ancient dam, its gatehouse roofs covered with pink tiles. A maze of tunnels and siphons lifts and drops and carries the water to a braid of canals that parallel the river as it heads toward Utah.

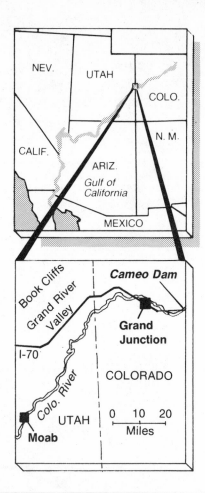

Some 60,000 acres are irrigated in the valley, mostly by small operators. Twenty-five acres of peach trees, which Talley owns, is enough to support and busy one man.

By state agriculture standards, the Grand Valley is not a major producer. Nonetheless, irrigation here illustrates how significantly agriculture affects the Colorado River.

Overall, 90 percent of the river is consumed by agriculture. By midsummer, when the spring runoff has passed, most of the water in the river will be diverted at Cameo for agriculture.

The most visible crop in the valley, the most picturesque, is fruit. But the most thirsty crops are feed for cattle: corn and alfalfa.

Here, as at every ranch I've visited on the river, more water than necessary is put on crops. On every acre of cropland, water several feet deep will be spread over the course of the summer.

Alfalfa, for example, needs about a foot of water per acre for each cutting. That same acre-foot will support a Denver family (with a healthy lawn) for a year. Corn needs 2 feet. Orchards need 28 inches, according to the Soil Conservation Service.

Yet I have seen otherwise conscientious farmers pouring 4 to 10 feet of water onto fields.

In the high mountain hay meadows, there probably is little damage from such flood irrigation. There is plenty of water, and what the hay doesn't use eventually drains to the river. I've even heard it argued that over-irrigation is beneficial because the soil stores water like a reservoir and releases it slowly year-round.

The difference in the Grand Valley is salt. Left in the shale by an ancient sea, the salt is dissolved by excess irrigation water and leaches into the river.

Where I first drank from the Colorado, in a hole in a snow-bank below La Poudre Pass, the water contained 50 milligrams of salt per liter — a trace. By the time it reached the Cameo dam, the river had picked up 400 milligrams per liter, largely from natural runoff and huge salt springs near Glenwood Springs. That's just under the federal standard for drinking water.

In the Grand Valley, every irrigated acre contributes about 5 tons of salt to the river. That could be reduced practically to zero if farmers used the minimum amount of water for their crop, plus a little to keep the salts moving away from the roots.

But irrigated-farming practices are a century old. And at $5 to $15 each acre-foot, water is a cheap, closely guarded property.

To reduce the salt in the river and meet federal water quality standards, the U.S. government is spending about $250 million in the Grand Valley to line canals to reduce leaching and to persuade farmers to reduce their water use.

I won't get into the stink the program has caused. But I will cite one statistic.

After all the money is spent, and assuming the best result, the government will have reduced the amount of salt in the river by just 15 milligrams per liter.

JUNE 28

He should have been a pirate, but he missed buccaneering by 300 years. He became a river rat instead. A rubber raft captain, seeking adventure on the high swells of rapids.

Fortune was forgotten. His life was afloat. "Let's go run a river" was his greeting and farewell.

When I first met Riley Dunn, I was put off by his swashbuckling. He was ribald, cocky and often bare-chested. His grin was maniacal, a row of rough teeth showing from a beard. One finger of his right hand was missing.

He wore maroon briefs — very brief — reinforced with leather where it counted when he rowed. A leather thong hugged his neck, tied through a hole in a stone.

"I found it on the Hoe River," he said of the stone. "I put it under my pillow and it gave me good dreams, so I kept it."

Before each float he would stand by the raft, wearing only his briefs, and christen the river:

"I pray to the river God, don't let the ranger find my body. I'd rather have some coyote eat me and make me a meal, than have some coroner tie my lips up through my nose and make me look happy."

In his 35 years, he had been many things a latter-day pirate might choose: smoke jumper was one he talked about. But since he was 14 he had been a river runner at heart. He lived in his van, he cared little for money.

I hired Riley to run Westwater, a fierce little set of rapids on the Colorado at the Utah border. Not until 1916 did someone dare try. It was the last segment of the Colorado to be run.

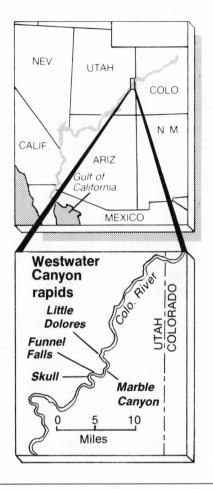

Since 1982, the river here had taken one life a year, out of 8,000 who run it annually. Bodies had been lost in the roiling water.

"I tell you what, this river is choice," Riley said as we floated away. "I'll bet it's running 18,000" cubic feet a second. Efa and Bill Daniels of Dolores were with us.

Riley talked of the rapids ahead, Funnel Falls, Last Chance and Skull. Skull was a left-hand turn with a man-eating wave. Caught by it wrong, we'd crash head-on into a wall. Or we could roll over it into the Room of Doom, an eddy surrounded by walls only rock climbers could escape.

A year earlier, on a raw Thanksgiving, I had taken a leisurely
float with Riley just upstream from here, from near Fruita
through Ruby Canyon, past Rattlesnake Canyon, to Mee
Canyon, where we camped.

It had rained buckets as we touched land, and it took us two
hours to get a fire going. Everything was wet, including the
inside of our tents. We slept in layers of clothes and froze.

Riley had dug a pit and buried a turkey in coals. We gnawed
it like savages and grunted. I hitchhiked out with Peruvian
sheepherders in gumbo up to my knees. But that's another story.
I knew that Riley meant adventure, so I came back this year
for more.

We stopped by the Little Dolores, a small muddy tributary
above the main rapids.

"Hike up, even 100 feet, and your perspective changes," Riley
told us as we tied the raft and walked away from the river
through desert.

It was sunny. A beautiful collared lizard, turquoise body with
a yellow head, ran at our footsteps. The flowers were vivid in
their desert solitude.

We climbed up a butte, tough enough for a rope belay, to
an island in the sky. Way below the river ran. I heard my first
canyon wren. Delta-winged cliff swallows whooshed by our lunch
spot, black and white flashes doing aerobatics for fun.

This was Bureau of Land Management property, virtually
unknown and unvisited, with arches, black ravines, brown ridges
and green spots of life.

Riley, wearing his briefs, boatman sandals and a pair of
bright, shredded gaiters, stood on overhangs that scared me.

"How far down is it?" Bill asked.

"Oh, 300 feet," Riley said. "The neat thing is that no one's
been here before."

We roped down and got back in the raft. The first splash was
breathtaking.

The canyon walls were black basalt, wet looking and sculpted.
Below us, I knew, swam the humpback chub, which was also
the name of the outfitter Riley worked for.

We ran one rapid, then two. The river calmed between high red cliffs.

But, in Riley's eyes, I could see the rapid ahead.

"I'll tell you what," he said quietly, pushing the oars. "This river is high."

As we entered from the right, I watched the wave build. We were sideways to the river and Riley rowed for his life. "Aargh" was all I heard above the rapid's roar.

We swept left with the current, the eddy passed by, then the buttress with a pileup of water at the base.

In a moment it was over. The rest was cake, and we took turns rowing to the takeout.

Riley lay out on the edge of the raft and looked up. Black birds soared above.

"I'd rather be a raven," he said. "They hang out in all the cool places. They play. They know they're here long enough to have a good time, then they're fat in somebody's belly."

He grinned his maniacal grin.

JUNE 30

Robin Wilson was a quiet guide. Not the kind to babble on, reciting names and history.

She was subtle in a land that was overwhelming: arches, monoliths, monuments of red, the country swept clean between.

She asked whether I wanted to visit a favorite spot of hers in Arches National Park. But she was silent as we drove in past Three Gossips, the Tower of Babel, the Parade of Elephants. What names!

Even at Balanced Rock, precarious cliché of the West, she said nothing and stayed in the car while I craned my neck and took pictures.

Down a dirt road, past the Fiery Furnace, we parked and walked the slick rock, following signposts of stone where thousands of feet had failed to wear a path.

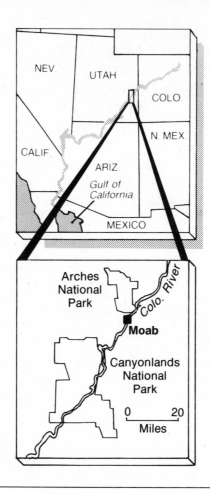

Years ago, Robin's late husband, Bates Wilson, had been superintendent of the Arches park. He was a man known for his Jeep and Dutch oven and love for Canyonlands.

"Bates had a very simple way of getting people into this country," Robin said as we walked. "He'd say, 'Hey, I'm going to such and such. You want to go along?' People were enthralled."

Bates hired as his first seasonal ranger an Easterner named Edward Abbey, and left him alone. The result was the book *Desert Solitaire.*

But Bates was best known as the father and first superintendent of Canyonlands National Park, next door to Arches. He wrestled from old uranium country, full of miners and cowboys, extractors by nature, a preserve no one could ever know fully, immense as it was.

Yet Canyonlands, I was learning, is an intimate place, each crack a small canyon, each scallop a little arch.

We walked past small gardens of blow-sand and rock, a pool of water, a cliff rose past its prime, a juniper twisted in death. It was, Robin said, as if each piece had been placed.

"These holes," she said, "Bates used to tell the girls they were made by rock rabbits."

When she and Bates married in 1970, they honeymooned in the new park with National Geographic. Bates took his Jeep, his Dutch oven and seven people, including the magazine's staff.

"That was typical of our lives," Robin said. "The stream of visitors at the Wilson house, the number of people wined and dined in six months was in the hundreds."

It was a second marriage for both. He was old enough to be her father.

She stooped to feel the sand and let me walk ahead, up a path carved by dynamite by an old miner Bates had hired.

I turned a corner and saw Delicate Arch. It sprang from the rock at the edge of a bowl, rough hewn in sandstone, not so delicate, really.

I tiptoed with others to the base of the arch. We stood beneath, trying to fit it all into a single camera frame, with a tiny person in the shadow.

Robin tucked herself in a corner in the warm rock, hugged her knees, and was quiet. A breeze blew her curly hair, graying in front.

Through the arch we could see, snowcapped, the LaSal Mountains. They rose behind the Wilson ranch in Professor Valley. A creek ran through, down to the Colorado.

"There were a couple of years, after Bates died, when I wondered whether I should be doing something to preserve an attitude," Robin said. "He was not a person who wrote things down. There is very little of his legacy in paper. I was very hesitant to be a spokesperson for that period in his life."

She received 300 letters after he died in 1983, which took a year and a half to answer. Time to mourn, time to realize that what she wrote in the notes, things he might have said, she believed herself.

And so, with another woman, she formed the Canyonlands Field Institute — "a carrying on of an attitude, of wanting this country understood and enjoyed."

The institute sponsors treks in the backcountry, nature walks and raft rides, a slide show of canyonlands that runs in Moab.

"As CFI developed, something began to happen inside," she said. "I'm now somebody who runs an enterprise that does something on its own — not just a leftover from someone else. I'm my own entity. It isn't something I have to hang onto, or line up the way he would."

We sat until the stone got hard, then walked to the car following the cairns. She picked a tiny flower and sniffed. It was sand verbena, most fragrant and attractive at day's end.

"Bates didn't go around pointing out things all the time," she said. "He allowed people to discover it themselves. He let those things come from within."

JULY 1

The script rested in the pickup seat beside me. As I waited for the director to shout "Action," I read the first page.

"Ext: Desert-Daybreak. Bold red rock cliffs stand in stark relief against a backdrop of high, purple mountains, their summits still delicately powdered with snow. The rays of the rising sun drift slowly, gently across the waking landscape, lifting night's curtain."

I closed the cover. I could see that mountains weren't the only purple thing in the script. I'd never get writing like that past my editor.

But this was Hollywood, sweetheart. I was on location with "Nightmare at Noon," about to make my screen debut.

"Action," the voice crackled on the radio. The '60 GMC pickup lurched forward into camera range.

Making movies in Moab goes back 38 years when John Ford filmed "Wagonmaster" with Ben Johnson and Ward Bond. The wagon train crossed the Colorado River near Locomotive Rock, just upstream from here.

In 1950, Ford returned with John Wayne and Maureen O'Hara to make "Rio Grande"—viewers never suspected the film showed the wrong river.

Since then, Moab has had a steady run of movies, television episodes and commercials: Cars atop thin buttes, sci-fi space scenes on the moonscape of Canyonlands, river scenes galore. Even the town dump has been filmed for its "beauty."

In a town as depressed as Moab, the filmmakers bring welcomed money. A Grade-B movie like "Nightmare" dumps a few hundred thousand dollars in a few weeks.

"The Moab Film Commission busted hump to get us," said Kirk Ellis, the executive producer. "Moab has a wonderful look."

Local people were hired. The police chief was one of the bad guys. My driver in the scene was Larry Campbell, a former miner hired to be location manager. But he looked so authentic, they put him in the truck with me.

Local people also have parts in a real-live drama going on in the Moab area. It is a drama that was reported by Edward Abbey in his book *The Monkey Wrench Gang,* which details the exploits of a group who terrorize developers.

Sold as fiction, the book is veiled history. The characters, the sentiments, the locations are real. The canyonlands of southeastern Utah are America's environmental battleground today. The villains and heroes fight on the 6 o'clock news.

The scenes in the book, in which the gang sabotages road machinery, are all true, said Cal Black, a San Juan County commissioner.

He is portrayed as Bishop Love in the book. Black is a real-life point man for development. He pushes for more roads in the national park, condominiums on Lake Powell, and a radioactive waste dump.

"Environmentalists—they're extremists, they're cultists," Black said. "I think I'm an environmentalist. I love this country, but part of the lifestyle is having a job to enjoy the environment."

Opposing Black is Ken Sleight, resort owner, backpacker, book store owner. He is portrayed as Seldom Seen Smith in the book.

"The canyons are a religion to me," he said. "You can touch the rock, you can hike up a canyon. You can feel it on your feet. It engulfs you. It's bigger than you are. But you can feel it completely. That's why you can come to a point and say enough is enough."

For Sleight, enough came when Lake Powell flooded Glenwood Canyon.

"The Monkey Wrench Gang is making a stand right now," he said.

Flying over Canyonlands, one is struck by the absolute rawness of this land. It is largely untouched, undeveloped.

But there are plans to change all that, said Clive Kincaid of the Southern Utah Wilderness Alliance. He points to a strip mine proposal here, a carbon dioxide plant proposal there. The alliance now is fighting the paving of the Burr Trail, a dirt road to one of the big marinas on Lake Powell.

Kincaid lives in Kanab, historically a film center like Moab.

Robert Redford testified in Kanab in opposition to a coal-powered electric generator. The townsfolk burned him in effigy. Whether there is a connection, Kanab is not the film center it used to be. And if *The Monkey Wrench Gang* is ever made into a movie, as is planned, feelings in southern Utah will run high again.

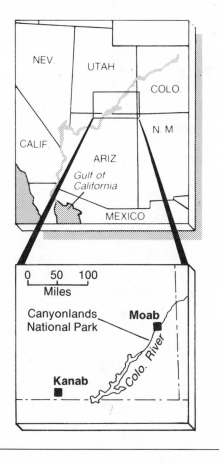

In "Nightmare at Noon," starring George Kennedy, an evil gang poisons the Moab water supply to drive people crazy. An actor and actress, Wings Hauser and Kimberly Beck, try to escape. But their futuristic RV breaks down and they hitchhike. That's when Larry and I pull up beside them.

As the camera whirred, Larry told them to get in back. I, dressed in my funkiest cowboy shirt and tractor cap, watched from the passenger side. I'm not even sure the camera could see me in there, trying to see around the truck's mirror. In disgust I picked up the script.

"Ken nods gratefully and motions for Cheri to follow, clumsily climbing up into the truck bed. He extends a hand down to Cheri, who carefully removes her designer shoes before boarding."

Larry shook his head at me and spoke into the rear-view mirror, fitted with a microphone.

"City folk," he said.

Watch for me in a theater near you.

JULY 5

When Tex and Millie McClatchy offered to put me up, I had no inkling they meant it. Not until I climbed the stairs, up the roof, three stories up, did I understand.

The view was terrific. So was the wind. My bed was on a plywood platform above their log house. If I had broad-jumped from my bunk, I might have hit the Colorado,which ran swiftly below, heading west through a gap in the canyons.

Somehow the accommodations fit Tex and Millie: open, outlandish, a bit of Texan overdo. Hustlers with heart. River people.

They lived on the river, they made their living on the river. Their 10-acre compound, seen from my perch, was a boneyard of their enterprise. Boats and buses, beat-up jeeps, an airplane, a carriage, canoes, rafts, and down on the river, in a levee of sand, their pride and joy—the jetboat.

They represented Moab, Utah, in the best sense. It was a town of survivors, peopled first by Mormons. The town was named for the Biblical Moabites, the people who live in the far country. Moabites today drive jeeps in national parks, mine potash or prospect uranium. After work they'll look you in the eye and tell you they're conservationists.

"Go where you want to live and get a job," was how Tex came to Moab, teaching school at first, then taking tourists through the strange land of canyons and buttes, desert and river.

"There were no national parks when I came here. I used to fly 'em one day, and raft 'em one day and jeep 'em one day. As tourism picked up, I gradualy quit teaching. This road gets woolly right about now."

He drawled as we crawled down a road meant for mountain sheep. He was loaded with canoes and a group that planned to paddle the still water of the Green River to the confluence of the Colorado. He'd pick them up there in his jetboat.

From that point to the sea, the river has always been the Colorado, named by the Spanish for the red silt in it. From that point back, the Colorado used to be called the Grand River—the stem I have been following. That's why everything along it is Grand something: Grand Lake, Grand Mesa, Grand Junction.

But in 1922, in a political coup, Colorado talked Congress into a name change, and the river became the Colorado all the way to Rocky Mountain National Park.

Either way, it is a powerful river here, navigable by powerboat—most of the time. The day Tex and Millie launched a paddle wheel, it stuck on a sandbar with the governor aboard. Tex and Millie were the crew, with an old vaudeville marimba player for entertainment.

If Millie were telling that story, she'd stop talking only to laugh. She is a big woman with long gray hair, and she seems bigger than life when she's talking.

"I tell people Millie can talk a cat off a fish wagon," Tex said the next day aboard a jet boat. "The river, to us, is outdoors. And it's free flowing. We're serendipitors. My days like to run loose. I run loose. There's no fences. I can go anywhere, anywhere I want to."

We roared through the red canyons, past chiseled cliffs and pictographs, jeep roads and canyons. The river winds, as does the Green, before they join, doubling their might. Tex's collie lay on the bow.

"This is my favorite view on the whole river," Tex said, cutting the engines and drifting by a huge horseshoe bend. Dead Horse Point was off to the north. We could see tiny tourists looking at us.

Down the river, Tex cut the engines again and we pulled into a stone overhang and stepped off to make camp.

"This is where I sat and designed paddleboats and jetboats," he said. "Right here where I don't have any disturbances."

I walked down the river rock to find a flat place. I wanted to be alone.

The setting sun painted the low canyon wall across the river. It looked like a battlement against the darkening sky.

There was a time, just a thousand years ago, when men made this their home. The Anasazi, the ancient ones, who built high homes in the rock, nearly impossible to get to, to guard against some enemy. They farmed the riverside.

For reasons not really known—drought, enemy, social decay—the Anasazi disappeared suddenly, leaving corn in their cribs, pottery and art scratched or painted in the canyon varnish.

I chose a night spot on a high rock, flat and facing upriver, with a cliff behind me, protected.

The river was smooth and quiet now, broken occasionally by a boil from the bottom. A light wind washed my face, and a canyon wren sang overhead.

I woke with birds, alive in the tamarisk, but I slumbered until the sun came up, turning the river to a liquid mirror.

Beside my rock slab, yellow princess plumes reached high to my nose. It was so quiet I could hear, overhead, a pair of raven wings beating. The sun made it hot as I sat in my skin and took it all in.

I thought of the Anasazi again. All along the river, I had seen abandoned homes, cabins, ranches. An abandoned uranium plant sat just outside Tex's place.

Each was a dream lost or moved on. Life is a process, not a goal, I've come to feel. Moving like the river.

JULY 6

The hefty man in shorts shouted, "Don't be too long. That tour boat could be here anytime."

He waved at a group tripping away in swimsuits and sandals and eased into a lawnchair inside the big, blue houseboat.

"There's 14 of us," he said, snapping open a drink. "Five couples and four kids."

Glenn Van Houten of Tucson had maneuvered a rented, 50-foot craft through narrow canyons to Rainbow Bridge, and docked, with only a little shouting, at a space marked "Tour Boats Only."

Now, 300 yards from one of the seven natural wonders of the world but troubled by his parking spot, he elected to forego visiting Rainbow Bridge.

"I don't need to see it," he said.

I walked through his houseboat, which rented for $1,500 a week. I counted two tape players, seven ice chests, 10 chairs, 11 fishing poles, five air mattresses, two windsurfing boards, a water ski, chaise lounges galore and four parasols tied to the top deck.

"All the toys," Van Houten said. "We firmly believe he who dies with the most toys wins."

Around us, along every available foot of dock, boats were tied. Houseboats, ski boats, even a sailboat dragged here by the Van Houten crew behind a jetboat.

The creation of Lake Powell paved a water road off the mainstem of the Colorado right to and under Rainbow Bridge. The lake ended centuries of isolation for the arch, a spiritual retreat to the Indians, known by the Navajo as the "rainbow turned to stone."

It could have been one of the golden arches for all the hubbub. As my daughter, Amy, and I walked to the bridge, a family was jumping into the water below it, swimming and shrieking at each leap.

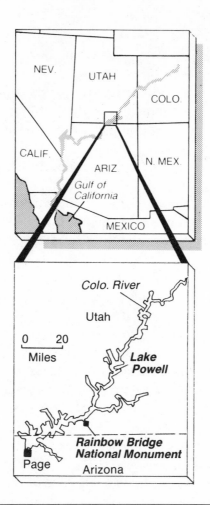

We walked back to the dock, watched a man use a mop to keep a houseboat from banging the dock. We left. Boats hurried by.

We motored downriver to the Dangling Rope marina, said to be one of the busiest gas stations in the West. Every day an ocean-going tanker brings gasoline to the marina to refuel boats. Twenty gallons cost us $30.

On any given day in the summer, hundreds of houseboats, plus hundreds of cruisers and outboards, ply the waters of Lake Powell. Each year, 1.5 million people camp on its shores, about 6,000 people a night.

Only 3 percent of the 1,900-mile shoreline is considered prime beach, and people are beginning to complain about the lack of good beaches.

"It's getting like camping," said Norma Heyer from Lakewood, who rents a timeshare houseboat. "If you don't start looking for a campsite at 1 p.m., you might not get the one you want."

Still, there are uncrowded arms of the lake. We rented an outboard from the new San Juan Marina, a Navajo venture on the San Juan River. There was little traffic until we reached the confluence of the Colorado.

The tribe wants to create two or three marinas on its land on the south shore. The National Park Service also will soon double the capacity of the Wahweap Marina near Page, Arizona.

The lake could handle more boat traffic, the park maintains, but the boat ramps and marinas are too congested.

Heading upriver, we passed a big boat flying the Colorado flag. Then another with a huge crowd of kids dancing on the deck. I couldn't hear the beat above my own motor.

Almost all the houseboats were dragging one or two out-boards, much like recreational vehicles pull cars. They use smaller boats to ski, visit canyons and make runs to the store.

Past Cathedral Butte, we pulled into Cathedral Canyon, out of the wind. The walls grew sheer. Brown, tan and pink sandstone disappeared into the green water. The walls closed in. I turned off the motor and the boat drifted into a little pocket.

What looked like steps carved into the sandstone spiraled upward to the sun above. Maidenhair fern grew in the first four steps. They may have been Moqui steps, carved by Indians to get into Glen Canyon.

Amy climbed out of the boat and lay down, a girl's young outline against the warm, curved sandstone. I wondered where the steps went below.

Up the river, we pulled into Music Temple Canyon, hiked on the sandstone, then cooled off in the quiet lagoon. We were out of the wind and away from the traffic. We could see a small arch to the west.

Below us, under water, was a canyon visited by Maj. John Wesley Powell on his Colorado River expedition August 1, 1869. According to a lake guide, Powell's men "camped here, sang songs and carved their names in walls of a 'vast chamber.'"

Flooding that chamber created a lake and a lesson. It's a lesson about water development in the West. Every project is a compromise. There are gains and losses.

Creating Lake Powell prevented the flooding of Echo Park in Dinosaur National Monument. It also created a lake of unsurpassed beauty, a navigable, stark wilderness of water and stone. Millions now see country that only a few hundred may have seen before.

But Lake Powell flooded a canyon that Maj. Powell had found stunning in its beauty. The people who catalogued its features before the dam was closed still are shaken over what was lost.

What they see today, in the exposed rock above water line, is only the forehead of a covered sphinx. I hope the roar of engines and clink of cocktails and top deck dancing, all the fun Lake Powell creates, does not drown the lesson, too.

LEE'S FERRY
TO
OVERTON

JULY 9

On a spot below Lake Powell, where the river runs green and cold, I arrived at the halfway point of this journey. Lee's Ferry, Arizona, is roughly 700 miles from where I started on the Continental Divide. To the Mexico border, the map says, it's another 689.

But Lee's Ferry marks more than just the middle of the Colorado River. In a very real sense, it is a divide between two very different kinds of country.

Gone are the last views of snow-covered peaks. The river, which has dropped 10,000 feet, runs through desert from here.

Gone are the streams fed by the snows. The major tributaries have added their water. The river below Lee's Ferry will grow no more.

Historically, Lee's Ferry was a place to get across — the only place in hundreds of miles of canyon cut by the river.

Too wide to bridge, too deep to ford, the Colorado kept a big chunk of the West a secret for centuries.

It turned away the Catholic conquistadors from the south in the 1500s. They thought at first that the river made California an island.

Three hundred years later, the river stopped the Mormons from the north, although they probed each finger of each canyon for settlements.

When John Wesley Powell ran the river in 1868, most maps labeled the territory "unexplored."

Powell, and nearly every other explorer, stopped on the Colorado near the Paria River, between the end of the redrock country of Glen Canyon and the polished sandstone of Marble Canyon.

Here, 15 miles south of the Utah border, the steep walls backed away enough to get in a wagon. Here, John D. Lee, a Mormon, began a ferry in 1871. It ran until 1928 when the arched Navajo Bridge leaped the cataract.

But Lee's Ferry is still the only accessible spot to the river. Every float trip through the Grand Canyon begins here, down a paved boat ramp to the water's edge.

I came to Lee's Ferry to see a mundane cable strung across the river nearby. Hung on it is a cable car, operated by the U.S. Geological Survey.

Once a month, a USGS technician wheels himself out over the river and drops what looks like a bomb into the water. The bomb, 100 pounds of lead, is attached to a cable. On the cable is an anemometer-like instrument to measure the river's velocity.

The rotating wheel sends clicks to a headset worn by the technician, who times them and measures the river's flow.

The technique hasn't changed substantially in 64 years of measuring the Colorado's flow at Lee's Ferry. The technician's work backstops an automated reading that is telemetered by satellite to Phoenix every four hours from a tall concrete tower across the river.

When measured last, the river was 398 feet wide, 25 feet deep and running at 8,730 cubic feet per second.

Over a year's time, the measurements equal the river's total flow.

From the mountains of Colorado, Utah and Wyoming, from a quarter million square miles of the West, the waters have come.

Seventy percent of the water comes from Colorado, 15 percent from Utah and the rest from Wyoming. It is an arid region, with an average precipitation of 10 inches. As a result, the river is rather puny by river standards.

The Colorado averages under 15 million acre-feet of water a year, with a range of 5 million to 25 million. The Columbia River empties 185 million acre-feet into the Pacific. The Mississippi is mighty, indeed, with an annual flow of 463 million acre-feet.

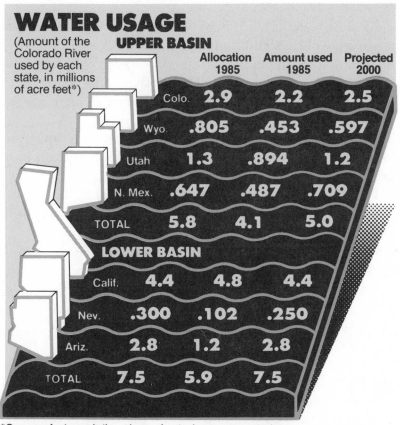

WATER USAGE

(Amount of the Colorado River used by each state, in millions of acre feet*)

UPPER BASIN

	Allocation 1985	Amount used 1985	Projected 2000
Colo.	2.9	2.2	2.5
Wyo.	.805	.453	.597
Utah	1.3	.894	1.2
N. Mex.	.647	.487	.709
TOTAL	5.8	4.1	5.0

LOWER BASIN

Calif.	4.4	4.8	4.4
Nev.	.300	.102	.250
Ariz.	2.8	1.2	2.8
TOTAL	7.5	5.9	7.5

*One acre foot equals the volume of water in a square container one foot high with a base one acre in area, or 43,560 cubic ft.

The USGS measurements are vital in determining how the Colorado's relatively small flow is used.

In 1922, a compact signed by seven states and ratified by Congress, gave half the river's water to the states above Lee's Ferry and half to the states below.

Unfortunately, the agreement was based on measurements in wet years. Since the compact was signed, the river's flow has been less than anticipated.

Up to now, that hasn't been a problem. Only California is using its full share.

As more water is used, however, the vagaries of the compact language will be significant. The so-called Law of the River dictates that the upper basin states, Colorado, Wyoming, Utah and New Mexico, get shorted if the river runs short.

The lower basin states, California, Nevada and Arizona, will get their full share.

Lee's Ferry marks the legal divide between the upper and lower basins. For me, it marks the beginning of a trip into a new territory.

I left Lee's Ferry thinking what Powell said at this point in his journey: "We are now ready to start on our way down the Great Unknown."

Maybe a little melodramatic, but I am eager to explore the second half.

JULY 12

Not far below the south rim, my mouth dry as cotton and my arms burning in the sun, I knew I had made a mistake.

We should have started the hike to the river, to the bowels of the Grand Canyon, at first light. By 9 a.m., it was hot as Hades and getting worse.

My daughter, Amy, photographer Susan Biddle and I were hiking down the Bright Angel Trail to meet boats for a float trip through the Grand Canyon. We carried packs with enough stuff for a week's camping. I felt like one of the mules that passed us, carrying tourists.

The mules left the steep, winding trail littered, smelly and difficult to walk.

People we met coming up were red-faced and dry. Only one, a baby being nursed by her mother in the mesquite shade, seemed content. I drank often from one of the water bottles I carried.

The switchbacks were interminable. It was only a mile to the river as a stone drops, but nine miles by trail. We hoofed it, afraid of missing the rendezvous. The thought of climbing back out was chilling.

A blister formed early on each foot; I stopped to cover them with moleskin. I pushed Amy to drink as we sat in the shade of Indian Gardens. We were, perhaps, halfway.

Back in the sun, we splashed across a creek and bent to cool our faces. The relief disappeared in 30 paces. We crossed water again and wet our hats. Then the creek left us in the desert and took a more direct route to the river.

Down through time we pushed ourselves. It seemed a snail's pace when I turned to drink and look at the rim behind us.

The river had run this course at an even slower pace — an inch a century. Down through the sediment of a sea bottom it dug, as the sediment pushed up to form the Colorado Plateau.

The weathering that formed the width and grandeur of the canyon continues as it has for 10 million years.

We came to the Devils Corkscrew switchbacks. By now, the sun was high and cast no shade. I leaned the pack against a rock to rest a moment and drink. We were in a solar cooker. The granite was hot to touch.

After three hours, we finally could see the river. It was flowing green and wide. It looked like a stream from above. What the Spanish thought was 6 feet across when they looked down on it four centuries ago was more like 300.

I wanted to wade in, but our path turned right. Uphill! I swore, but it only made me thirsty. I yelled at Amy to drink more.

The pack hurt. The path leveled. Someone we met sent word from Susan, who had walked ahead to flag the boats. Keep going.

We crossed sand, hard to walk in and scorching. The Kaibab suspension bridge appeared, but seemed to hang out there, never closer. I was nearly through my second bottle of water and exhausted.

The river is mostly calm in the Grand Canyon, giving the author time to reflect and talk with boatman Mike Davis. Photo by Susan Biddle

We crossed the bridge and stumbled onto the beach. The packs fell off. Someone gave us water and led us to the river, so cold it was shocking.

What a contrast, this cold in a furnace. The water that flows from the base of Glen Canyon dam 90 miles upstream is 46 degrees. It kept beer fairly cold in the boat holds, and I had one.

Amy was dehydrated, white and weak. She came back slowly, sitting in the water. Susan, rejuvenated, helped us pack our stuff into rubber bags. None of us could eat.

We joined an expedition that had been on the river five days from Lee's Ferry. Twenty people in five wooden dories, each with a boatman. A raft carried food and camping bags.

By this time, everyone had stripped to canyon basics: swim-suit, shirt, sneakers and first names. Many of the men had five-day beards.

Our gear was stuffed in hatches somewhere. We strapped on life jackets, found empty seats and pushed off. Amy went with someone I didn't know and had to trust.

We floated, rocking gently, past the desert sands we had crossed. I was happy to sit and watch.

I don't remember much about the next few hours. We floated, rowed, ran a few rapids and pulled into a sandbar thick with tamarisk, a wispy bush of light green and little shade.

The routine, we were told, was to find a flat spot and claim it for a bed. Our bags were wet, and we spread them on the bushes to dry.

The kitchen was a spread on a tarp, two tables were unfolded, and cooking was begun.

We were lectured on the "unit" — the pot that was nothing more than an oversized ammo can with a toilet seat balanced on the lid. Separate paper from waste. Pee in the river. Wash your hands.

Crew leader Mark "Moqui" Johnson blew a conch shell. Dinnertime.

We sat around in the sand and made friends, and talked over the constant roar of Granite Rapid, which was just ahead of us.

Tomorrow, we were told, we would get what we came for, a day of whitewater in the Grand Canyon.

JULY 15

From our campsite, the brightly painted boats drifted into the quiet water, moving slowly toward the unmistakable sound.

The boatmen stood to read the water. They pushed their oars for position. The roar grew louder.

We hitched our life preservers tight, shifted to balance the dory and hung on. The anticipation was like climbing that first big hill in a roller coaster.

The water warped downward. The boats, turned sideways, slipped over the edge. White froth erupted.

We tipped from side to side and end to end. Sheets of cold water drenched us.

Like crashing through a surf next to a cliff, we rode through Granite Rapids. Up, down, then up again. In a minute the churning subsided, and we looked for the next one.

Hermit Rapids came straightaway. Our dory must have tipped 60 degrees on one wave before plunging into the next one. The water came in. We laughed as we bailed.

Running rapids is crazy fun. The ultimate ride is on that edge between thrill and disaster. Someone dies just about every year in the Grand Canyon trying it. Seventeen thousand make it.

In a sense, the rapids here are waterfalls over boulder dams. Each rapid was formed by rocks tumbling from side canyons during flash floods. Water backed up behind, much like the water in a millpond, before churning over the rocks.

The granddaddy of all the flash-flood rapids is Crystal, next on our list. Formed in 1963, it has eaten more than its share of boats and people. The boatmen made us walk around while they ran empty.

Next we rode the "jewels," Sapphire and Ruby, Bass and Shinumo. By now we were old hands at this.

There are 160 rapids in the Grand Canyon, accounting for half the 2,000-foot drop between Lee's Ferry and Lake Mead. But they account for only 9 percent of the 255 miles of river.

The rest is quiet water, a gentle float if you have time. Most raft companies buzz through, using motors. Our boatmen rowed us, like Cleopatra on the Nile.

I looked around. We were an affluent bunch: bright boys from law school, an orthodontist and his daughter, two professors, a nurse, an architect from Germany, a Toyota dealer from South Africa.

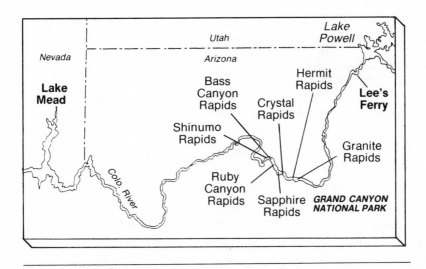

Bob and Kit Moore never had camped before. She sold boilers in Louisville.

Steve Rabinovitz, a Boston broker, was so new to the world outside his office that he worried about getting his shoes wet.

We camped for the night on a huge sandbar, clean and untracked. Maureen Mundt, the cook, made burritos, and after dark, boatman Pete Gross got out a guitar and sang below a three-quarter moon.

In the morning, we had avocado and shrimp omelets. Then we hauled the boats to the water which had dropped several feet.

The river in the canyon rises and falls like a tide each day, as water is released from Glen Canyon Dam to generate power for Phoenix. Boaters sometimes must wait to run a rapid.

The bigger effect of the power tides is on sediment, the basic building material for life in the canyon. The dam shut off 85 percent of the sediment that created the beaches in the canyon. The tides eroded much of what remained.

Tamarisk moved in, along with an explosion of birds in its branches. The canyon adjusted, for the moment, to man's daily power cycle.

We pushed off, and it started to rain. We pulled on ponchos. As we floated the gloom of Middle Granite Gorge, Pete played his recorder—"Raindrops keep falling on my head."

That night we ate steaks and drank wine. The next day we hiked to Thunder Creek, played like children in a water slide, and ate lunch below a thunderous waterfall that erupts from a hole in the canyon wall. The spray created an oasis of cotton-wood, monkey flower, grape and watercress.

Walking back, I lingered to talk to Mike Davis, one of the boatmen. Something was bothering me.

Bearded, gentle, the unofficial medic, Mike had rowed 15 years for Martin Litton's Grand Canyon Dories. Mike and his wife, Marilyn, another boatman on our trip, were outdoor professionals. They taught skiing in winter and rowed dories in summer. They made it look easy.

That, I told him, was my problem.

I had come to the Grand Canyon expecting a wilderness trip. A journey into a strange and desolate world. Dangerous, maybe. Unsettling, certainly.

Instead, we were on a catered camp. We ate like kings and queens, we were looked after, pampered, handed beer when we wanted, led on hikes, told where to jump into warm side pools and steered through killer rapids with finesse.

I suppose for $100 a day, we should expect that.

But, I wondered, had floating the Grand Canyon become just another vacation for those with enough money?

It began to rain again and to hail. We ducked under a ledge.

Mike didn't answer directly. He showed me an Anasazi ruin, a sacred Dactura plant, used by Indians for hallucinations. He talked of uptight people who unwound in the canyon.

What he said came down to this: give it time.

That night, the storm left us. Big fleecy clouds raced across a bright moon, which painted the canyon black and gray. A last lightning stroke froze the rapid below us in a brilliant white moment.

The best rapids ride is on the edge between thrill and disaster. Here the dories Okeechobie (above) and Phantom (below) ride rapids. Photo by Susan Biddle

The canyon became a huge observatory, open to the sky in an ancient arch. We lay at its bottom and watched stars. There were billions.

I tried to remember what day it was and how long we had been on the river. I couldn't.

JULY 19

Each morning in the Grand Canyon was a new painting, a creation of rock and rising sun, river and sky.

As the desert haze burned blue, the smell of perking coffee would stir us, and we would go to the river to bathe.

The water had turned cocoa from the rains, but was not any warmer. Washing took will.

Amy and I went out in an inflatable canoe to battle the rapids. They were riffles to the boatmen, but they tossed us. Then we floated, drifting through the Granite Narrows, hiding in the rocks from the others.

By now, I liked smooth water as much as the rapids. There was time to look, to think.

We drifted past a hundred overhangs. Lizards did push-ups on vertical walls, and desert bighorn sheep tiptoed down talus slopes.

We pulled into Matkatamiba Canyon, narrow and deep. We walked through the warm trickle of water until the canyon narrowed to our shoulders. Then we climbed.

Kit Moore, who only two days earlier had turned back from a scary hike, crawled gamely. At the top, her husband, Bob, stretched out in a bathtub carved in the streambed.

The rest of us lined up across the trickle, creating a "butt dam" to block the warm water.

After a week in the canyon we had lost our city pallor and our inhibitions. Even Stan Goodenough, the very British South African, joined in our informality.

Bob Moore leads the way into Matkatamiba Canyon, one of many side trips in the Grand Canyon. Photo by Susan Biddle

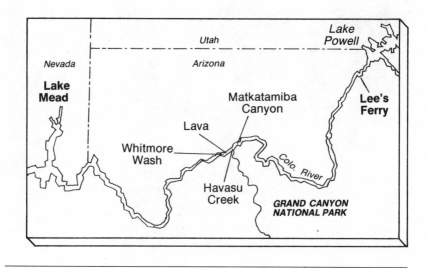

Stan was accustomed to safaris at home. While laboring with a pack one day, he cracked: "At home I would have a bearer."

Stan said he recently had been divorced, having endured until the children were grown. He called this trip a sojourn. "I have resolved to grow: physically, mentally, spiritually," he said.

It's funny how we travel to find things inside.

Later that day, Steve Rabinovitz, a Boston broker, sat with me in a dory and eloquently described the canyon's effect on him.

"I used to be so regimented. I was worried about camping, about my shoes, about my bowels. But I sleep better here on the sand than I have in years. No headaches.

"I have everything. A house in New Hampshire, a phone in my car. I belong to the club. I go every night. My kids are in private schools, with exorbitant tuition.

"I live in a world that runs by the hour. But here, time is measured in years. When you look at what time has done it gives you a whole new perspective.

"I used to be in a hurry. I used to battle companies. Now, I think I'll let time create the advantage."

We pulled into Havasu Creek to spend the day in the magical riverine canyon, swimming, jumping off ledges, lost in the jungle of foliage that filled this place.

I walked ahead, thinking of what Steve had said. I needed to be alone.

I splashed through the crystalline water, past grape vines and waterfalls that drowned out all else. I found a huge rock in the stream and climbed to its top.

For me, this trip was more than an assignment. It was one last chance to be a father to a girl who was growing and going away.

Amy, who is 12, would soon leave the Rockies to move with her mother to New England. I would not see her as much. I needed this trip with her.

Our last day in the Grand Canyon took us through Lava Falls, and I had arranged to ride a dory with Amy and photographer Susan Biddle. Ted Toth of Austin was the fourth passenger, and Marilyn Davis our boatman.

For a couple of days the boatmen had hyped Lava as a fierce little ride, the toughest in the canyon, they said. The last big rapids on the river.

After Lava, it was a short ride to Whitmore Wash, where we would be picked up by helicopter and flown to the rim.

We pulled off above the rapids to look at them. We were told we could opt to walk around them. No one did. We had grown accustomed to riding.

Our boat went last to allow Susan to photograph the others. One by one they ran it, down a slot, through two standing waves that filled their boats with water, and out. It looked routine.

Once through the main waves, each dory rocked through more turmoil as the river headed toward a wall on the left. Across the way was a beach, our home for the night. Each boat pulled in, and passengers got out to watch us.

We buckled in and Marilyn pushed off. Ted and I were in front, the heavies to lean into the waves if they should threaten to roll us. Amy and Susan were in back. Everything was stowed.

Time — and life — take on a new dimension in the Grand Canyon. Photo by
Susan Biddle

We rolled down the slot and into the first wave. We were turned slightly to the left and it hit me first on the starboard bow. As water poured over me, I pushed into the wave. The boat leveled and we were through, full of water.

The boat was still tilted forward when the second wave hit us. It towered ahead and slightly to the right. I looked up at it, a brown wall with a frothy head, and leaned into it. But it ripped my hands from the gunwale and all I saw was water and the boat coming over me. We were flipping.

We had been briefed for this moment. We had been told to come up on the upstream side of the boat, hang on to lifelines strung around the bottom, and then pull the boat over and climb in.

Whatever sense of up and down I had, though, was lost in the rapids. The life jacket brought me up by the overturned boat. My first instinct was to grab it. The second was to find Amy.

I looked to my right and saw Ted, Susan and Amy in a row on the lifeline. Amy's face was white.

"Hang on," I yelled.

"I'm trying," she said. Susan had one hand on the boat and one on Amy's arm.

Marilyn was missing. I remembered our instructions. I tried to loosen the flip-line buckle to begin the climb up. But nothing stood still long enough. We were bobbing through the rapids, water dousing our heads. It was tough just to hang on and not get banged.

While I tried to figure out the buckle, I thought of rocks, but felt none. I don't remember being cold.

Another dory loomed out of the waves. Mike Davis had rowed out with Jon Graham to help. By now Marilyn was on top of the overturned boat and yelling to us. "Turn it over. Get in the boat." The wall was coming.

Jon jumped in and pulled with us. The dory came over, slowly, then with a rush. Jon pushed Amy in. Susan climbed in. I struggled to pull myself up. Ted got in and helped me.

Camping on narrow sand bars in the Grand Canyon makes close friends of strangers. Photo by Susan Biddle

"Bail," Marilyn yelled. We were wallowing and headed for the wall. We bailed, and Marilyn pulled us clear.

Within a minute we were on the beach, snapping open beers and exulting in our survival. The rest of the group stood around, and we told and retold every little detail, every bump, every scary moment.

"We're a little jealous," said Stan, and we all laughed.

It had been a picture-perfect rescue. Amy had come up away from the boat. People on shore said Susan had pulled her in.

On shore, Amy was still shaken. I took her away from the jabbering group, and we sat in the sand. She told me what she remembered and felt and slowly unwound.

That night, we had a campfire that we were reluctant to leave. The boatmen handed out medallions made from tin can tops and strings. I received one for losing my glasses to Lava Falls. Amy got one for snoring through a rapid sometime earlier.

Finally, we walked to a high spot we had chosen for the night. It looked over the camp, Lava Falls upstream to our left, a shadowed cliff across from us, and the river moving off to our right, toward the flat water of Lake Mead.

At last the canyon had touched me. I knew now that the river still was in charge and that wildness, though tempered by dams and catered groups, was still here.

I hugged Amy and lay down, thankful that we were alive. I started thinking, what if? but shook it off.

A warm desert wind blew across our faces and we soon fell asleep under all those stars. It was our last night together in the Grand Canyon.

JULY 22

There is no mistaking the end of the Grand Canyon. The deep walls part, the brown silt sinks, the green water turns blue, and the Colorado, having coursed its last wild reach, is stilled.

Were it not for Lake Mead, which backs up the river, the scene would be no different from what John Wesley Powell saw when he, five men and two boats emerged from their pioneering trip in 1869. There is a sense of relief and anti-climax as civilization reappears.

Today, you see houseboaters, water skiers and bass fishermen. Powell was met by Mormons from St. Thomas, one of Brigham Young's southern colonies at the confluence of the Muddy and Virgin rivers. They had been sent to look for wreckage and bodies, but instead celebrated Powell's success with bread, cheese and watermelons, bounty from their irrigated farmland.

St. Thomas lies beneath the lake today, but its Mormon tradition and descendants live on in Overton, the village that took its place upstream on the Muddy.

The valley is a green spot in an inhospitable desert, typical
of Mormon communities in the West. While the Indians may
have pioneered irrigation, the Mormons raised it to a fine art —
and a religion.

Brigham Young believed that wisdom evolved from husbandry
and that irrigation fulfilled the prophecy of Isaiah, who said that
when Christ returned "the desert shall rejoice, and blossom as
the rose."

In the first days of the church in Salt Lake, the pioneers found
they could not even turn the soil without first wetting it. They
build a diversion dam across City Creek, plowed and planted
potatoes and wheat. The next year they dammed Big Cotton-
wood Creek and ran a series of canals to each ward. Each bishop
was appointed watermaster for the ward.

It became standard practice in each Mormon town to dam
and divert water through ditches plumbed with crude surveying instruments. One bishop sighted across a broad milk pan
filled with water to find a ditch's course.

As their methods became more sophisticated, the Mormons
learned by trial and error how much water to divert for different
soils and crops. Mormons subsequently wrote the books on irrigation. By the time the federal Bureau of Reclamation was
created in 1902, the Mormons were irrigating 6 million acres.

To this day they hold influential positions in the bureau, which
built the major water works in the West. Today the bureau is
building the Central Utah Project that will divert water from
the Uinta Mountains, part of the Green River-Colorado system,
to Salt Lake's basin.

The work, while not openly tied to the Mormon faith or talked
about much in modern church services, nonetheless has a solid
foundation in Scripture. Their work, Mormons believe, is
preparatory to the coming of Christ.

In Overton today, farmland is being reduced gradually by
suburban growth. The town is becoming less a Mormon farm
community than a bedroom town for Las Vegas, an hour away.
Yet the original water rights remain, as do the ditches that run
to the farms and the village.

People with shares of water receive by mail a monthly log for water use. The log lists the time their water will arrive in the ditches. It might be at midnight, and the permit may allow only six minutes of diversion, but the homeowner faithfully arises and waits for the stream to roll toward him. At the appointed hour he sticks a tin or shingle into the stream to divert the water into his lawn or garden.

It is truly a life stream, for Overton receives two inches of rain a year. "It's not enough to talk about," said Karl Marshall, a Mormon farmer. "A lot of people get more in one evening than we do" all year.

Marshall farms year-round, using each acre for two crops: green onions, radishes and tomato transplants on his farm outside of town. It was very hot when I visited him, and we sat in his darkened living room and talked. He was a big, gentle man with rough hands.

I told him that along the river I had seen attitudes and water practices that defied logic, common sense, even facts. Money was spent to irrigate land that then required more money to drain. Dams were built that were not used, or benefited few. Water literally ran uphill toward money.

And at every point along the river people acted as if the river were theirs, a parochial fervor that reduced their neighbors to water bandits. It was almost, I told Marshall, as if water in the West were a religion.

"It is a religion," he said without hesitation. "You've got to fight for it or die. You've got to make it your religion."

On my way out of town, I stopped to talk to one of the Mormon bishops, a fellow named Ivan Cooper. He worked in a silica plant, his house was centrally air conditioned, and he farmed a small plot behind his house, mainly as a hobby. He said water never came up in Sunday services.

But out in front of his suburban home, water was running as I left, warm and clear through the concrete ditch. I went back to Isaiah and read:

"In the wilderness shall waters break out, and streams in the desert. And the parched ground shall become a pool, and the thirsty land springs of water."

LAKE MEAD
TO
THE GULF OF CALIFORNIA

JULY 24

W atching the pros weigh in their bags of bass, I didn't feel so bad. Two, three, maybe five pounds of fish tipped the scale. Ten pounds in two long days wasn't unusual. Some of the best had been skunked, just as I had been.

I had stumbled onto a U.S. Bass tournament on Lake Mead, a gathering of fishing wizards with whizbang gear, men who spent their lives hooking largemouth bass for big bucks. They traveled the country, pulling special bass boats with monster engines, radar fish trackers, depth finders, swivel seats and foot-pedal trolling motors. Rigs worth $20,000.

Some of the professionals on the tour made $200,000 a year, just fishing. The money came from endorsing products, names they wore on bright badges sewn to their shirts. They were walking billboards for lures and line, electronics, boats and motors.

Lake Mead had always been a favorite spot for them, the biggest fish, the biggest tournaments. Bass heaven. I had to try it.

I hopped a ride with Tom Reed, a U.S. Bass editor, on the company's carpeted fishing platform. The Mercury 175 pushed us through the waves, through Boulder Canyon, to a quiet cove. Tom turned on the radar. The descending bottom traced a line. Above it a school of bait fish cast an electronic shadow. Between the two, almost certainly, lay the big ones.

Tom handed me a rod with a squiggly fake crawdad. He fished spinnerbait, the choice of last year's champion. He stood in front, controlling the troll. I cast from the back into the clear water. I let it sink, reel and sink, just like a real crawdad would swim.

All over the lake, in secret spots, the pros were doing the same. They had been at it since daybreak, plumbing the depths for the fish they had scouted. The bass showed as inverted Vs on their radar. The experts could actually watch their lure descend to the fish.

"It's not luck," said Mike Folkestad of Yorba Linda, California, winner of the U.S. Open on Lake Mead. "Fishing competition is totally professional, totally educated. Everything you have is a tool, and you learn how to use the tools. Then you've got to understand the fish. You learn how to follow the food chain."

But fishermen are finding that Lake Mead's food chain has a defect. The bass in Lake Mead are disappearing. The catch has declined from 800,000 fish in 1963 to 100,000 last year. Even among the pros, bass fishing is getting tougher.

The reason, according to biologist Larry Paulson, is that Lake Mead no longer receives the silt it once did. The Colorado River once dragged 130 million tons of silt into Lake Mead, threatening to fill it up in 100 years.

Glen Canyon Dam was built in 1963, solving that problem but creating another. Phosphorus, attached to the silt, was eliminated. While most other lakes in this country, subject to sewer and farm fertilizer runoff, nearly choke on the stuff, Lake Mead began dying for lack of phosphorus.

Without phosphorus, there was no algae. The clear water showed that. Without algae, plankton could not grow. Without plankton there was no threadfin shad. No shad, no bass. Even striper bass, which dominated the lake, were starving.

They were "two-and-a-half feet long and skinny as an eel," said Paulson. I could blame my empty stringer on something other than poor fishing skills.

A few days after the tournament I went back on the lake with Paulson, who directs the Limnological Research Center at the University of Nevada at Las Vegas. In May, he and 1,000 fishermen dumped phosphate fertilizer onto 30,000 acres of the lake. Within a month plankton had increased and schools of shad were once again showing on the radar.

To revive the lake, Paulson feels, fertilizer will have to be applied periodically. Meanwhile fishermen are dumping thousands of Las Vegas Christmas trees into the lake's barren bottom to improve the bass habitat and are contributing thousands of dollars to save their fishery.

They are man-made solutions to a man-made problem. Lake Mead is the largest artificial lake in the country. It holds two year's worth of the entire Colorado's flow, 27 million acre-feet, in a lake that stretches more than 100 miles.

And because it sits in a desert, its surface evaporates 6 to 8 feet of water a year — 600,000 acre feet a year, more than the Front Range of Colorado takes from the river.

When the lake was created as a reservoir for irrigation, power and water for burgeoning southwestern cities, no one envisioned its recreation use. But the very growth it created also spawned a demand for water sports, away from the crowds, on the river's fresh water.

Last year 8 million people visited Lake Mead, a lot of them water skiers, a lot of them from California. They spent $26 million at marinas and lakeside resorts, which is roughly half the revenue the dam generates in power.

But that doesn't count the money spent on boats, water skis, life jackets and beer. Or the unestimable value of a weekend away from L.A. The Colorado, for all its life-supporting wealth, may, in the end, have as much value as a respite from the civilization it sustains.

JULY 26

Somewhere in the belly of the behemoth the guide droned on with his spiel. "Hoover Dam is 660 feet thick at its base, 45 at its crest. It is 1,224 feet wide and is the highest dam in the Western Hemisphere."

I was listening to something else, the throb of water at the bottom of a lake 700 feet deep.

"You are standing in a diversion tunnel, 56 feet in diameter, which took 3.5 million pounds of dynamite to blast over a period of two years."

I began thinking about bodies in the concrete. I'd always heard that men had been buried in the dam.

"There are 4.4 million cubic yards of concrete in the dam, power plant and related structures. During construction, a 16-ton bucket was dumped every 60 seconds, around the clock for two years."

What an awful death, I thought, lost in a slurpy grave.

"Each pouring raised the dam six to eight inches, so the stories of bodies buried in the concrete are not true."

I snapped awake.

"Ninety-six lives were lost, from blasting, electrocution, drowning. There were 3,500 men on the job, and one dog."

People in the tour group smiled. There must have been 50 of us crammed in the tunnel, trying to absorb something of what the guide was saying. The numbers just kept coming, the benefits, the history, the height, the breadth, the water, the power.

Every day, 2,000 people take this tour, creeping across the dam to find limited parking to wait in line to visit a dam. A dam. In its first 50 years, 24 million people have gone through. I wanted to know why.

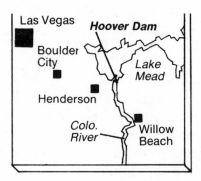

"It's one of the wonders of the world isn't it?" said Gordon Maurer of Berwick, Pa., who was standing next to me. "A year ago we went to the Houston Astrodome. We enjoyed that."

Maurer and his wife were on vacation, on a mission really.

"I had a friend who died of cancer three or four years ago," Maurer said. "That made up my mind. We're going to see this stuff—Mount Rushmore, the Grand Canyon."

He isn't the only tourist to lump together God's creation with man's. In most people's minds, I think, Hoover Dam is a bit of both.

"It was a thing of great importance," said chief guide Tom Gailey. "People have heard about it all their lives."

Bigger dams have been built, even more graceful dams. But 50 years after its birth, this sweeping arch between the rough, dark walls of Black Canyon is still embraced by America as no other.

"Hoover Dam was a winner in all aspects," said Julian Rhinehart of the Bureau of Reclamation.

It tamed the Colorado. It turned the river's delta into the richest irrigation project the world had known. It watered and powered Southern California. It provided jobs in the Depression. It was a public work of public respect.

I have not read one environmental writer who has had the courage, or desire, to criticize Hoover Dam.

Hoover also established the way future reclamation projects would be paid for. Power would be sold to pay back construction costs.

Hoover can generate 1,900 megawatts. Half of it goes to Southern California. When Hoover was first built, it provided 97 percent of Los Angeles' power. Today it is only 3 percent. Running full bore, Hoover could have provided about half the power Colorado used during one of the hot days last week.

With new generators, revenue is expected to be $50 million a year, double what it had been for the first 50 years when power sold at half a penny a kilowatt/hour. This year the rate doubled to a penny, compared to commercial rates of 2.5 to 5 cents.

Hoover Dam is lit at night by the power of the river that runs through it.
Photo by Jay Dickman

Dams like Hoover are considered cash registers for reclamation projects. Most of them subsidize irrigation. Some pay
money into a fund for future dams. But reclamation payback
is a political game played by Congress, with cues from the
Bureau of Reclamation.

Not so long ago, two dams were proposed in the Grand
Canyon — dams that would have flooded Marble Gorge, lower
Havasu Canyon and Lava Falls — to generate revenue and power
for the Central Arizona Project. Those proposals were defeated,
but bureau literature still speaks of the untapped hydro power
potential of the Colorado.

Some portions of payback are interest-free over 50 years, with
no regard for the declining value of money. Hoover's interest
is 3 percent.

Hoover's original construction cost of $165 million was sup-
posed to have been paid off in 50 years, as of June 1 of this year.
But along the way Congress deferred a chunk of the payback,
and tapped some of the revenue for other things: the Arizona
Project, a new visitor center at the dam, and new generators.

The result is that Hoover Dam, the pride of America, won't
be paid off for another 50 years.

JULY 28

I woke sometime in the middle of the night, 3 a.m., maybe 4,
to the persistent whine of an outboard motor. I pulled the drape
and looked out. There was another ferry, crossing the Colorado, with another load of gamblers.

As I watched, the boat plied back and forth between the casino
dock below and a parking lot across the river, Arizona to Nevada
and back again.

The river glowed yellow from the lights of the bar below and
the neon sign above me. "Tanya Tucker" it flashed. "Slots" and
"Chicken buffet $2.99." The river, which runs hard and smooth
past Laughlin, was just another attraction.

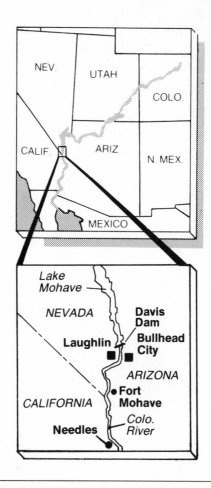

Downstairs at this hour, somewhere among the dinging machines, Don Laughlin walked, surveying his dimly lit kingdom. Gray-haired and thin, pasty-looking and rich, Laughlin had turned this desert riverside into a gambling mecca.

Starting with a rundown bar, he had built a $75 million business on the strength of ma and pa gamblers in RVs and people from Arizona and California turned off by Vegas 100 miles away. The Postal Service eventually named the town for him, but Laughlin still worked as hard as he ever did, until 5 each morning.

When Laughlin arrived in 1966, there was little but sand on the Nevada side of the river. Today, there are half a dozen casinos and a hell-bent-for-leather spurt of development by other casinos hoping to steal, or add to, Laughlin's thunder.

While I was there, Circus Circus opened the Colorado Belle, a casino shaped like a huge riverboat, and the town board approved a complex of four more casinos with 6,100 hotel rooms and a golf course. A 17-acre riverside lot next to Laughlin's casino was on the market for $30 million.

Altogether, the town board has approved zoning for 15,000 hotel rooms and homes for 24,000 people in a town without a town hall, and a post office stuck behind the quarter slot machines in the Riverside Resort.

"I think we've only scratched the surface," said Laughlin, a small-town Minnesota boy who bought his first slot machine from a magazine ad when he was 11. He quit school in the ninth grade when the principal complained about his $400-a-week business of operating slots in local bars.

That, in time, took him to Vegas, where he tended bar, went to dealer's school and bought a small-time bar with a gambling license. But he wanted a spot on the state border, and he found the river. Now his ferries haul 150,000 people a month for what he calls the "adult carnival" of gambling.

I have never understood the allure of gambling. But what fascinated me in Laughlin was the unbridled development in a desert land.

While the river flows by, cool and inviting, Laughlin can use only 10,000 acre-feet — about eight hours of the river's flow — for the entire year. That's what Nevada has left to take from the river. The rest belongs to somebody else downstream.

That means that the town can grow only so far and must decide between casino rooms and homes for casino workers, who number in the thousands for each resort. Two hotel rooms use as much water as one home.

So far, amid all the dust of construction, the casinos are winning. Workers have to live on the Arizona side of the river, in Bullhead City, which has twice the water.

Don Laughlin, who owns 5,000 acres of land on the Arizona side, built his own bridge across the river for $3 million, but then couldn't open it to traffic because of a dispute over maintenance. It just happens to cross by his hotel, which despite the new competition, is full year-round.

With typical Sun Belt zeal, Laughlin's town board has approved more development than it has water for. Chairman Ted Finneran, who works in a casino, said to me: "You can't turn them down because you think you're going to use up all the water. You cannot control trade that way. I see Laughlin continuing to grow until we run out of water. It's who gets there first."

Laughlin, in a small way, is no different than the other boom cities of the Southwest. Los Angeles didn't have any water either, but developers convinced politicians to do what was necessary to get it. Phoenix followed suit.

After hearing about his ranch, his planes, his helicopter, his cruises, his good-looking girlfriend, and his take, I asked Don Laughlin if he had everything he wanted.

"Does anybody ever have all he wants?" he replied. Then he paused.

"I'd like to set my age back about 30 years," he said. "I'm 56 years old. Oh, I have my health. I'm just sorry I'm not younger."

JULY 30

Somewhere in the desert, on a stretch of hot road, a sailboat rode by on the back of a truck.

Its sails were furled and its mast pulled down. As it pulled out of sight the heat formed a line of blue below the hull and made waves where the truck bed had been. For just a moment, the boat was afloat in a desert sea, an optical illusion in a land of little else.

The river nearby offered nothing to please the eye. Small dry towns, backwater refuges and miles of sluggish water lined with tamarisk. Below Needles, Calif., it bent through its last canyon, Topock Gorge.

It was just a few miles more to the next optical tease — the London Bridge, spanning the waters of the Colorado.

After 16 years in America, the bridge had settled in. Trees had grown up around it, the grass had matured and the bridge looked as natural as anything around it.

A fake paddlewheel floated beneath, a fake English pub looked on, and kids played in its shadow with every water toy imaginable.

Up to now the bridges I had encountered on the Colorado had a more serious function than drawing tourists. They were built to cross the river, to advance civilization in the West. In 1,200 miles of river, I counted 70 bridges. Taken as a group, they represented the history of that advance.

The fallen tree was the most elemental, high in the Rockies where the spring runoff made it impossible to wade across the river. Men then improved on that by planing one side flat and fixing the ends so it would not roll. I remember sitting on one of those bridges in Rocky Mountain National Park, watching the river begin.

The first highway bridges added planks across two logs, then planks across steel beams. As the river widened, the bridges grew complex. Cantilevers reached beyond the pilings in the riverbed. Then trusses appeared, an American invention commonly seen on old railroad bridges where metal is erected above the bridge in a series of triangles.

The first suspension bridge I saw was at Dotsero, near the top of Glenwood Canyon in Colorado. Built in the 1930s, it is still used by the Golden Bair family to trail sheep across the river to summer pasture. It is a tiny thing, three feet wide, but classic in its shape.

For the most part, the Colorado is spanned by dull highway bridges. One of those has replaced a one-lane wooden wonder

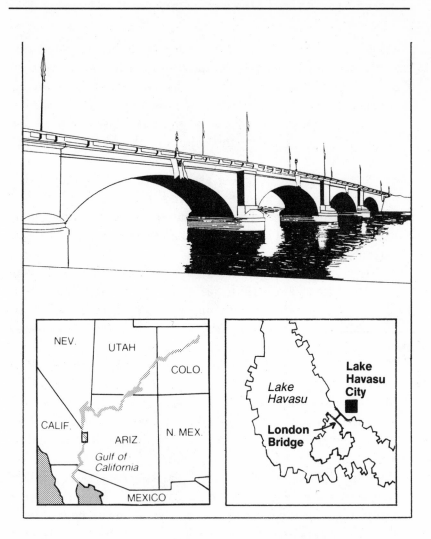

at Dewey, Utah, above Moab. The old bridge still stands, though, a tribute to the days when crossing a river was something to remember.

The London Bridge at Lake Havasu City is probably the only example on the river of the Roman arch. The bridge contains a steel and concrete core with the original stone as a façade.

After diving for lost tourist valuables, Doug Fisher comes up for air at the London Bridge on Lake Havasu. Photo by Jay Dickman

After it was built on a peninsula on Lake Havasu, a channel was dug across the peninsula under the bridge, making an island. Shops, hotels and condominiums sprang up around it, and the crazy idea of Robert McCullough, the chain saw magnate who developed Lake Havasu City, took on a life of its own.

As Joseph Gies says in his book *Bridges and Men,* a bridge is a place of life. Build one and roads converge. "The conditions that caused it to be built may change, but the fact that it is there forces life to come to it."

The bridge played a major role in the development of London. So, too, did it put Lake Havasu City on the map.

Today, 1.5 million people visit every year, including bus tours from England. After the Grand Canyon, the London Bridge is the second most popular tourist attraction in Arizona.

Not bad for an old bridge that was falling down.

AUGUST 2

Havasu Lake is a long drink of water, no matter how you measure it. Stretching 50 miles along the Colorado—from Needles, Calif., south past Lake Havasu City, Ariz., to Parker Dam—the skinny lake is famous for its warm, smooth water and hideaway coves and year-round boating.

But the real reason for the lake is the Southwest's insatiable thirst.

Near the end of the lake, white pipes that are 10 feet wide climb a hill from an imposing marble pump house and disappear. Like straws, they suck water from the lake.

A billion gallons of water a day is pumped into the Colorado River Aqueduct and uphill 250 miles to Los Angeles and San Diego. The Colorado provides two-thirds of the water for Southern California's 13 million people.

But that's only half the story at Havasu Lake.

Almost directly across from the California pumps, Arizona has built a system just as big that already is slurping up water for Phoenix. Scottsdale and Tucson are next on the canal. When the system is finished, water will run east across the desert for 335 miles, draining as much water as California from Havasu, for cities, Indian reservations and farms in the middle of Arizona.

While the two states share Havasu Lake, little love is lost between them. They have fought for years over the Colorado, mostly in court. In the 1930s, the Arizona governor sent his National Guard to prevent Parker Dam from being built. At the time, Arizona was mostly agricultural and couldn't afford to bring water from the river like Los Angeles could.

The Central Arizona Project changed that, and I wanted to see it.

I took off from the pump house to follow the water, a blue strip through a bleached concrete canal in the gray desert. I

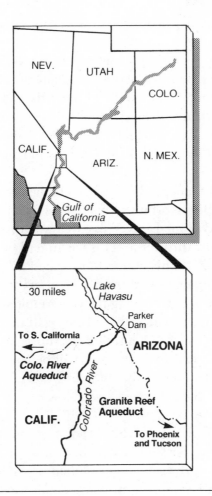

drove for hours. A gallon of water takes three and a half days to reach Phoenix.

Saguaro cactus and a tall fence stand guard the length of the canal. This is precious water, after all. At $3.5 billion, the Central Arizona Project is the most expensive water project in history.

Already the Colorado River is running into homes in the northern suburbs of Phoenix, a city that boasts one of the lowest water rates in the United States, $13 a month. As I drove through the streets, people were watering lawns and washing their cars.

Phoenix was built on the Salt River. For years, it took water for granted. The Sun Belt boom eventually outpaced the supply, and the city sank deeper wells to meet demand. That's when the Central Arizona Project came to the rescue.

Water then began to follow the people, rather than the other way around. The Colorado River is watering Phoenix's new growth.

"I think most people here refuse to believe they live in a desert," said Bill Korbitz, Phoenix's water director. When Korbitz moved from Denver five years ago, he left his lawn mower, his snow thrower and his ice auger behind. He hauled 35 tons of granite to his house and created a desert landscape.

The water department is pushing conservation. Under state law the city must stop lowering the water table by the year 2024. The state also has decided that urban water will have priority over agriculture. If the Colorado runs short, farms now receiving Central Arizona Project water will be cut off before cities.

Korbitz thinks eventually the safest, most dependable water source will be the city's own waste water, treated and run through the system again.

But in the meantime, Korbitz is going to the ends of the Earth to find enough water so that Phoenix, now 1.9 million people, can continue to grow. The city bought a whole valley of irrigated ranchland along the project's canal for $30 million.

Someday, they think, it will be worth the $300 to $700 per acre-foot that it will cost to pump it into the canal and push it to Phoenix. That is 10 times what Colorado River water will cost the city and 100 times what water costs now.

The economics may be a sign of things to come.

"No community is limited from a water standpoint — if you're willing to pay," said Korbitz. "We haven't even tapped Alaska. I don't laugh at floating icebergs off the California coast. Hopefully, the Colorado mountains will be loaded with snow."

AUGUST 3

One of the joys of traveling a river is discovering the unexpected. It happened often this sumer—just around a bend an interesting character, an issue I hadn't thought about, a town I'd never visited. Though many things were planned, I always left time for serendipity.

So it was that in the lower stretch of the Colorado I discovered wild life.

When I found it, I stopped long enough to study it, to immerse myself in it. I took an entire weekend, in fact, to make sure I understood it.

I rented a little recreational vehicle on the California side of the river, just below the Parker Dam on Lake Havasu, because I'd heard the view was good from there. I stocked up on groceries, with plenty to drink. It was extraordinarily hot. I slipped into some shorts and went out.

The river was alive with wild life.

A yellow boat, shaped like half a rocket, going about as fast and making twice as much noise, went by. A tail of water arced behind it.

A blue boat, barely touching the water, whizzed by in the other direction, pulling the arms off a skier, who dodged the first boat.

A gaggle of jet skis came swirling by, leaping the wakes of both boats, doing figure eights with themselves, the skier and someone floating by in an inner tube.

Each machine was louder than the next. Instead of back seats, most boats had 484 Chevy V-8s with straight pipes. In the front of one boat, a man drove, holding a beer with one hand and a bikini-clad woman with the other.

A man in a nearby trailer offered to take me for a ride in his boat. It was a racing model, not nearly as fancy as the sparkly ones on the river. It had two seats bolted to the hull, a steering wheel, an oversize foot pedal and an ignition key.

When he turned the key the boat lurched out of the water. The motor, a 484, was attached to the prop. He headed down the river. I thought he was going fast.

But when he turned around he stomped on the pedal and my eyes went out of focus. I don't know if we touched any water. But I was glad when he lifted his foot.

"That was about 60," he said. "We won the drag races at 140. In a quarter of a mile."

I thanked him and headed for Sundance, said to be a wild life refuge down the river.

I paid the cover fee at the door and walked into a room full of skin. Brown skin, Everyone was carrying a beer can.

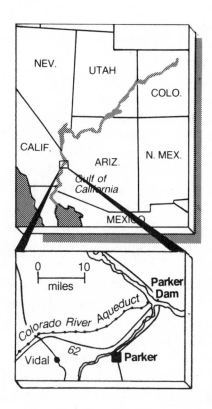

I heard a roar out front and walked down a gangplank onto a dock filled with people. They were yelling at a bunch of boats bobbing in the water. Specifically, they were yelling at women in the boats, who eventually responded by removing their plumage. Their top plumage. Then the crowd roared.

I watched for a long time. Until the hot leg contest started inside.

All of this, I later found out, was the Parker Strip, famous for what they call "river fever." Half of Southern California comes here on weekends, the half not at the ocean. They come in pairs in small pickup trucks, pulling a trailer with a boat. They camp cheek to jowl on the shore and, as they say in California, "party."

There are other wildlife and wildlife refuges on the river, but they aren't faring as well. For one thing, boat wakes swamp the floating nests of birds. Jet skis are a particular problem in little backwater areas used by birds to hide their nests.

"They get in there and rip around and flood the nests," said Will Nidecker of the U.S. Fish and Wildlife Service. "The eggs cool. The mothers abandon the nests."

The Colorado always was an important flyway for migratory birds. Spring flooding would create mud flats that would fill with hundreds of thousands of ducks and geese. After the river was dammed, three wildlife refuges were created to protect the backwaters.

The refuges, Havasu, Cibola and Imperial, run from Needles, Calif., to Yuma, Ariz., on more than 100 miles of river largely undeveloped. But the river here also is navigable, heavily used by boaters. It also is managed primarily for irrigation and power.

As Nidecker put it: "Wildlife is not a high priority for the Bureau of Reclamation."

As a result, the number of species in the wildlife refuges actually has declined.

In the 1940s, the bureau tried to dredge part of the Havasu Refuge, the northernmost refuge. More recently, it has channeled the river in the Cibola Refuge, "armoring" the levies south of Parker Strip with rock.

Finally, in the high water years of 1983 and 1984, flooding that was caused because the bureau's dams were too full for unexpected runoff devastated habitat in all three refuges.

The floods wiped out willow and cottonwood that supported more than 100 species of birds at Havasu. Killed, too, were cattail and bullrushes, which filtered the water and allowed the sun to generate new growth for ducks.

At Imperial, crop land that supported migratory fowl disappeared under water. Instead of thousands, only 450 Canada geese were counted this year.

"Our populations are down significantly," said Nidecker, who at night has watched flocks of birds pass the national refuge for better habitat somewhere else.

"They overfly the refuge," he said. "They don't even stop, unfortunately."

AUGUST 5

In the desert, the color green is a celebration of life, if only a solitary bush holding its own in the sand.

The sight of acres of plants is a triumph, by comparison.

One of the biggest swaths of green along the lower Colorado River is below the town of Parker, Ariz., on a long flat bottomland. Eighty thousand acres bloom in 40-acre squares, each square a picture of prosperity framed by water.

This is the Colorado River Indian Reservation, home to Chemehuevis, Mohave, Hopi and Navajo, barely 1,900 souls who hold in common a piece of farmland and a priceless water right.

Last year, with the market depressed, the land produced $50 million of alfalfa, cotton, melons, wheat, lettuce and other crops. The land could produce twice that, if it all were in production.

The tribe's water right is for 717,000 acre-feet of water, twice what Nevada gets from the Colorado and a quarter of Arizona's share. That's enough to pour 7 feet of water on the tribe's 110,000 acres of irrigable land, where crops grow year-round in the desert heat.

The water right is ancient, dating to the 1860s and '70s, when the reservation was created. The water is also cheap to use, flowing by gravity from a dam across the river upstream from the reservation.

But if you drive through the crops, down the paths along the canals, it is unlikely you will see an Indian face. In this horn of plenty, Indians are strangers in their own land.

Only 20 of the Indians are farmers. Most of the land is leased to whites, who cleared the land, dug the canals and, in return, paid cheap rates for high-value farmland—$15 or $20 a year for each acre. Last year, the tribe received $4.6 million from agriculture leases, which basically supported the tribal government.

Some of the big operators are from California's San Joaquin Valley. Despite rules to the contrary, they employ few Indians. Migrants are hired on a reservation with 40 percent unemployment.

When I asked tribal officials about this, they resented the implication.

"Why should we all be farmers?" was a common answer.

"That's what the U.S. government wanted, to make farmers out of Indians," said Bill Alcaida, a former tribal chairman who ran the tribe's 8,000-acre farm for 14 years at a profit.

The tribe's farm manager is Joe Sigg, a white man who left a Chicago trust company to help the tribe increase its farm income.

He is renegotiating leases, raising them to $85–$100 a year. He convinced the tribe to buy into a high-risk, high-gain deal for cotton. And he is trying to lure more big operators to farm on the reservation.

All along the Colorado, Indian water rights are some of the best, and some of the least used. The courts have ruled that when reservations were established, there was an unwritten but

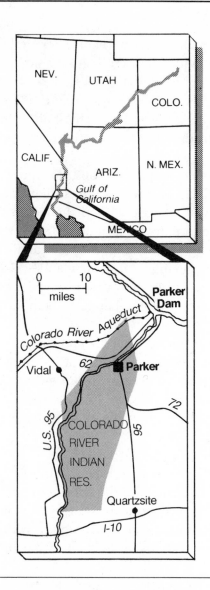

implied expectation for irrigation water. As a result, an enormous amount of the Colorado's water belongs to Indians; if fully
used, somebody will have to go without, or buy it from the tribes.

But, as one lawyer working on Indian water rights put it,
"Taking that valuable paper right and translating that to income
is a difficult task."

Developing water takes money and management know-how. Most tribes depend on Congress to pay for projects, whether it be irrigation canals or RV parks, and Congress has been slow to pay. Back on the San Juan River in Colorado, the Ute Mountain Utes have a good right to water but no way to get it without a dam and canals.

The Navajos, with the huge Navajo Lake to draw on, have so far put only 46,000 acres of land into production, half of what they could irrigate.

The Colorado River tribe is ahead of most tribes, using 70 percent of its water and the capital of outsiders to develop irrigation projects. The tribe has attempted, with mixed results, to develop recreation along its 90-mile waterfront on the river. Now it may hire another outside manager, like Sigg, to bring the riverfront to life.

"Agriculture is a springboard to other diversity," said Dennis Patch, a councilman whose grandfather remembered days when farming consisted of sticking seeds in mudflats along the river. He saw watermelons hanging from mesquite trees, lifted there by flood waters.

The whites "made their money, but we learned," said Patch. "Hopefully, we'll make ours from what we learned."

In Arizona, cities, not farms, will have first right to water if there is a shortage.

"The future of Arizona agriculture," Sigg believes, "rests with the reservation.

"Our message is, this is a good place to have a farm. This is like no other reservation. They don't need a dime of federal money. There's no reason they can't do it all."

AUGUST 7

My last boat ride on the waters of the Colorado occurred just
north of Yuma, Ariz. It was a short ride, with a U.S. Fish and
Wildlife ranger, to get a look at the stretch of slow-moving water
lined with giant cane and plugged with sandbars.

It wasn't a pleasure ride. I had to see the last stretch of what
still could be called a river. Down below us, Imperial Dam
changed all that, turning the waters of the Colorado into a
plumbing system.

Nearly all the water moves in canals away from the old riverbed, which the Bureau of Reclamation here calls a "sluiceway,"
a depository for silt drained from the canals. Dredges work 24
hours a day to clean the sluice of a million cubic feet of silt a year.

The giant share of the river goes west in the All-American
Canal to the Imperial Valley. The rest goes east to irrigate lands
along the Gila River, which is drained of its water in Phoenix.

Yuma was the site of the first dam on the Colorado, the first
Bureau of Reclamation project to turn the river's water to irrigation. That dam, built in 1930, is downriver from the Imperial
Dam, and Yuma still is a productive, year-round farm area
known for its citrus.

But the plumbing has gotten more complex over the years. The
bureau calls it "operating" the river with "hydraulic efficiency."

The canals run like a slot-car track, through straightaways
and curves, over and under each other, down through
generators, up through pumps. It's a surprise when someone
points out a levied waterway and says, "That's the river."

Even water that must flow into Mexico is diverted into the
All-American Canal first and dumped through a generator
before regaining its bed near the border.

Mexico indirectly is responsible for the Yuma area's grandest
plumbing device, a desalting plant that will cost more than $200
million to build and $25 million a year to run.

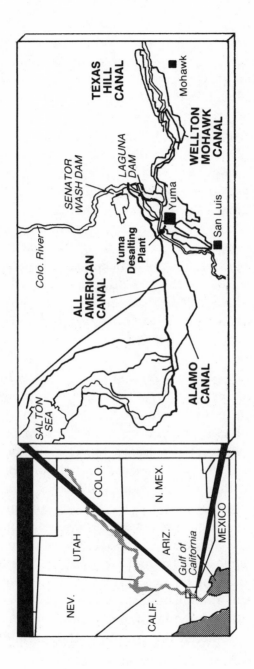

The plant is the Bureau of Reclamation's answer to a problem it created, and is an eloquent example of how man's attempt to bend the river to his will can result in a Gordian knot.

By the time the Colorado reaches Yuma it is very salty. The river carries 9 million tons of salt a year, half of it from natural sources.

I couldn't taste the salt in the river, but at Yuma it contains more than 500-parts-per-million salt, the recommended limit for drinking water. Above that the salt can cause erosion and plant burns. Under treaties with Mexico, the water flowing across the border must be no more than 115-parts-per-million saltier than what Yuma receives.

The farmland east of Yuma, along the Gila River, is very salty, and crops began to fail. The bureau drilled wells to pump the salty water out of the ground into a concrete canal which runs 50 miles through Mexico to the sea. The canal cost $23 million to build. The water in the canal is rank, about 3,000-parts-per-million salt, and 100,000 acre-feet of water is lost carrying it away.

The desalting plant will pump that canal water through high-tech osmosis filters and clean it to 285 parts per million, about as good as it is in the mountains back in Colorado. The plant's operation will consume enormous amounts of power.

But here's where it gets crazy. The clean water will then be mixed with the salty water in just the right proportion to meet the Mexican standard, no more, no less.

It would have been cheaper in the long run for the government to buy the irrigated land and take it out of production, as it did with 10,000 acres of the saltiest soil. But that solution ignores the upheaval of removing whole communities.

"Can you imagine the headlines?" one bureau official said to me. "You've got a whole bunch of real live people out there who have been making a living for two or three generations. There would be stories about the poor guy whose grandfather came here."

What is not headlined is that subsidized water irrigates surplus crops, which another arm of the government is subsidizing. The desalting plant lets that cycle continue, at even greater cost.

The best comment on the whole process comes from a Bureau of Reclamation fact sheet on the desalting plant itself. Under "benefits" is this line:

"Social and political benefits accrue that are outside the normal realm of economic quantification."

AUGUST 9

Say the word "farm" and an image comes to mind: a red barn, a man on a tractor, black and white cows, probably a silo, and a big old farmhouse.

That's the kind of farm I remember, the kind I worked on as a boy. My grandfather was a farmer. My father tried to be, but he tried just as the picture was changing, when big was better. So we lived on a farm leased to a neighbor. He had the big barn and the silo.

I say all this so that you'll understand my naivete as I headed west from the Colorado River toward the Imperial Valley.

It was late in the day, and the setting sun cast a rose shade on the sand dunes along the interstate. To the north, right through the dunes ran the All American Canal, carrying most of what was left in the Colorado River—about 20 percent of its total flow.

The dunes gave way to scrubland. On the Mexican side of the road, the border patrol was beginning a night's work, looking for illegal aliens.

Sixty miles west, the land turned green. On both sides of the road, the fields stretched as far as I could see. Signs on the fences told what grew there. Carrots. Asparagus. Alfalfa.

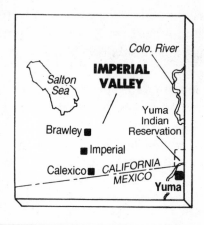

Then came the lights of what looked like a refinery. It was an alfalfa pellet factory, cranking out cattle food.

A little beyond, tractors were working with their lights on. Pickups were all over fields that were sculpted into ridges and squares.

I passed a fertilizer plant, bigger than anything I'd ever seen. A line 30 feet up on a big tank was marked "Sea Level." Then came a feedlot, full of dirty cattle.

Nowhere did I see a red barn. Nothing I saw looked like my image of a farm. Yet this was the most famous, powerful, irrigated farmland in America.

To me it seemed more like an industrial complex, pouring seed, fertilizer, pesticides and water into the ground. A 24-hour, 365-day, 500,000-acre factory producing food for the nation.

Every morning, farm managers called their orders for Colorado River water to the Imperial Irrigation District headquarters. There, men with calculators added up the figures and called the dams on the river. They ordered ahead because it took a week for water to get from the Hoover Dam in Nevada to the fields.

Once there, water was dispensed by 50 men, called zanjeros, who opened gates each morning. A night shift adjusted the flow. The water ran on each field 24 hours.

There was something about the Imperial Valley that, for all its fame and fortune, was old-fashioned. People didn't handle water much differently than anybody else. They just handled more of it.

I stopped at one "farm," the La Brucherie Ranch, and talked to the manager, Stan Mitosinka. He was jovial and tanned under a broad straw hat. Standing beside a commodity ticker, he reeled off figures as fast as the machine.

"We're down to 5,000 acres. We make a cutting of hay every 30 days. We cut and water every eight or nine days."

He had 1,500 acres in alfalfa from which he got 10 to 12 tons per acre. This year he planted 500 acres of Sudan grass, baled it, stuffed it into tractor trailers and shipped it to Japan.

There were 11,000 cattle in feedlots on the ranch, down from a capacity of 20,000.

The farm employed 30 people, 75 at lettuce-thinning time, about the only job done by hand with hoes. Most everything else was mechanized. The field crews worked night shifts.

A zanjeros tends to water running in ditches in the Imperial Valley, America's vegetable basket. Photo by Brian Brainerd

When I visited, they were just getting the fields ready for fall planting. Carrots would be the first in, in late August. Harvest would begin in January.

"We had 450 acres of lettuce this year. We get 24 heads to a box, 700 to 1,000 boxes per acre. That's a lot of lettuce."

They planted 600 acres of carrots, each acre producing 40 tons. There was another 400 acres of mixed vegetables, parsnips, rutabagas, turnips, leaf lettuce. And 300 acres of broccoli.

They fertilized like mad, 500 pounds per acre for lettuce, followed by two dressings. "Carrots, I load 'em with phosphate to get that orange color. Oh yeah, we also grow Imperial sweet onions, too."

The ranch also employed an entomologist full time to kill bugs.

The farm grossed $1 million just on lettuce. "But you take all your costs out . . ." Mitosinka held out his empty hands. "By the time you get to net, that's a different picture. You're left with a few dollars."

We smiled at each other.

"Every month we're harvesting something," he said. "We're not that big. We're just a good average biggie."

AUGUST 12

She was doing her wash when we pulled up, dipping her thin hand into a bucket of blue soap and rubbing it on the clothes. She scrubbed back and forth on the chunk of concrete that was her washboard, then rinsed the soap off in the canal.

She was sitting near a ladder, made of scrap lumber and wire, that lay against the sloping concrete wall of the Alamo Canal. She used the ladder to reach the water. She washed as she talked, speaking in Spanish.

Her name was Juana Rosales. She and her family were squatters, *paracaidistas,* which translated means, roughly, para-

Juana Rosales carries water for her garden from the Alamo Canal in Mexico. Her family "squatted" along the waterway and built an adobe house. Photo by Brian Brainerd

chuters, dropping out of the sky. They had built an adobe home from the earth along the canal, dipping water with a plastic bucket to mix mud. Her husband and son-in-law thinned cotton in the irrigated field across the canal for $3 a day.

They had a small garden by the house, a row of corn and squash, which they irrigated with the bucket. Some of her nine children and 12 grandchildren lived with her.

They swam in the water to cool off, they drank from it, they watched dead animals float by. Sometimes, she said, "it tastes like rotten mud."

In Mexico, as in the United States, the Colorado River mostly flows in canals. But nowhere on my trip did I see a more poignant connection between water and life.

All along the canal people had crowded in, living in homes of adobe, cardboard, car parts and cane. Under Mexican law, squatting is allowed on unused land. "When we came there was nothing," Mrs. Rosales said.

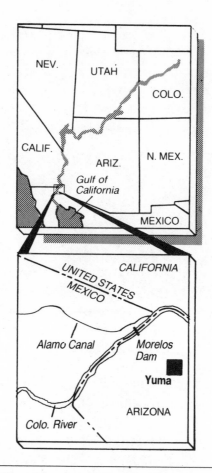

The Alamo Canal begins at the Morales dam near Algodones, in the state of Baja, Mexico, just across the border from Yuma, Ariz. Morales is the last dam on the Colorado River, and the point at which, on many days, the river goes dry.

The dam is a common crossing point for Mexicans trying to sneak into the United States. They wade across, swim across, even walk across the dam, and follow the river to Yuma. I saw several groups of young men crouched on the river bank, waiting for dark.

Under a treaty, the United States must release 1.5 million acre-feet of Colorado River water to Mexico each year, and under normal conditions not one drop more crosses the border.

Since 1983, however, an estimated 50 million acre-feet of water has flowed into Mexico because U.S. dams were full and the river was high. The resulting floods in Baja forced many families along the river to new homes along the canal.

I asked Mrs. Rosales if she knew where the canal went.

"Only God knows," she said, waving downstream. "It just goes."

For many miles, the canal parallels the river bed then curves off to the west, to irrigate farmland that grows much of America's midwinter fruits and vegetables.

The bottomland between is rich, and Mexico has colonized it with small farms. I stopped at Ejido Pachuca, a farm collective, and talked to one of its pioneers, 70-year-old Leonardo Balderrana.

Years ago, he said, they pumped water from the river, but that changed when the river went dry.

"Americans have dams," he said. "So they only send water according to the treaty. Here we were forced to use the wells."

At one time the ejido's land belonged to a big American company. Balderrana and 38 other farmers were able to move in at no cost and, with rural bank credit, begin farming 50 acres apiece. He bought John Deere tractors in Yuma, Ariz., and in a good year made almost $10,000.

He put four children through college on his farm income. Two became electrical engineers, one was a teacher and one an accountant. His son, Juan, is the ejido's mayor.

"We are supporting our families," said Balderrana. "We are educating them. We are producing."

AUGUST 16

The wind whipped the silt into a whiteout as we edged off the dike onto the mud flats. The wheel tracks we followed disappeared in the swirl, then reappeared when the wind died.

The silt sifted into the jeep, coating everything—our glasses, our skin, the cameras that photographer Brian Brainerd carried. It was a fine layer of the Grand Canyon, washed here over centuries and ground to dust.

I followed the tracks for miles, peering into the diffuse light. Solitary sets of tracks led off the main road, grinding through the soft surface. They were braver souls than I.

We passed dried driftwood, bleached as skeletons. Tufts of grass waited for water. Without warning, the mud flats dropped into the river. I veered away and stopped.

I was a little surprised to find the Colorado River looking so normal, wide and muddy, cutting through the delta. I had heard stories that it no longer ran this far, across a strip of Mexico's Baja, into the Gulf of California.

I stepped down the edge into muck up to my knees and walked into the water. It was salty. It was sea. The Colorado here was as much ocean as river, an estuary in a no-man's land. The tide was coming in.

We saw it first, then heard it. A wave, like the surf on a beach, coming up the river. It washed over sandbars, chewed at the mud on the side. It stood three feet high and just kept coming, churning up the riverbed at 10 miles an hour.

When it hit me, it felt like the surf. But rather than recede, the water stayed high and kept rising. The water pushed past me, up river. The Colorado running backward.

This was a tidal bore, the result of the tide narrowed by the Gulf of California and jammed into the riverbed. It is a phenomenon seen in only a few places in the world, a couple of them in North America. Historical accounts said the Colorado's bore at times had knocked over boats.

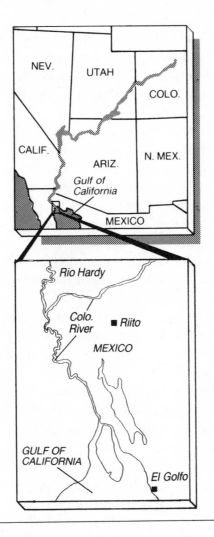

So it appeared that the water in the river here was part tide-water, part irrigation runoff from Mexican fields, part salty water that had made its way 1,400 tortuous miles—down 14,000 feet from the Never Summer Range in Colorado to the sea.

We got back in the car and headed downstream. I wanted to find the spot where the river met the gulf. The wind picked up. We kept running into muddy sloughs, left from fingers of sea. We had to go around them. Soon we were making our own tracks in a wasteland without a horizon.

This was not a place to get stuck or run out of gas. It could be weeks before someone showed up, and we were a long way from the last humans — squatter fishermen who built their camps, with names like Campo Los Amigos, on the river upstream.

We had stopped to talk to them earlier. They told us of the flooding in 1983, when the delta, the great wide deposit of Colorado silt, had sprung back to life. The water had flooded their camps for three years. When it receded, the bottoms of aluminum trailers were gone, eaten away by the water.

Since then, the river had dug a new bed, going where it wanted, one last fling at being wild.

We turned around. The river was getting wider, the sloughs soupier. If there was a place where the river officially ended, I couldn't find it.

We followed the tracks, up on the levy, back to Riito, then south toward the sea. We drove out of the silt storm into blue sky. To the west, the mountains of Baja were silhouetted by an afternoon sun.

We could see the gulf curve toward the river's mouth. A dozen shrimp boats lay anchored there. We drove into El Golfo, a little fishing village on the east side of the gulf.

The streets were sand, green nets were stretched between trees, and children played in the surf. Fishermen in broken English told us what they caught, holding their hands apart in the universal language of fish length.

I couldn't resist getting my feet wet again. The waves came in, one after another, without end. It was a beautiful way to end a trip.

There is something eternal about the sea, and the river, too.

Far away to the west I could see water rising into clouds, moisture that would blow inland someday to the mountains of Colorado. There it would begin this journey all over again.

Photo by Brian Brainerd

Appendix: annotated guide to places to visit along the Colorado River

Headwaters to Kremmling

Rocky Mountain National Park
Estes Park, CO 80517
(303) 586-2371

north on US 34 from Grand Lake; fishing, hiking, ghost towns

Grand Lake Chamber of
  Commerce
14700 Hwy. 34, P.O. Box 57
Grand Lake, CO 80447
(303) 627-3402

fishing, sailing, power boating

Arapahoe National Forest
240 West Prospect
Fort Collins, CO 80526
(303) 482-5155

for campsites along Lake Granby

Town Hall
Hot Sulphur Springs, CO 80451

quiet resort town

Bar Lazy U Guest Ranch
Parshall, CO 80468

Williams Fork Reservoir
c/o Division of Wildlife
6060 Broadway
Denver, CO 80216

gold medal fishing

Upper Colorado River

Bureau of Land Management
455 Emerson Street
Craig, CO 81624
(303) 824-8261

white water rafting and canoeing
information for the stretch
between Kremmling and Dotsero

Colorado River Outfitters
    Association
P.O. Box 20281
Denver, CO 80220

Glenwood Canyon

Amtrak
413 7th
Glenwood Springs, CO 81601
(303) 945-9563

information on the train that runs
through the canyon

Glenwood Springs Chamber of
    Commerce
1102 Grand Avenue
Glenwood Springs, CO 81601

hot springs, lively white water,
Glenwood Canyon hikes

Hotel Colorado
526 Pine Street
Glenwood Springs, CO 81601
(303) 945-6511

listed on the National Register
of Historic Places, Hotel
Colorado is completely restored
to its 19th-century charm.
Complete European health spa

Hot Springs and Vapor Cave
I-70 and Grand Avenue
Glenwood Springs, CO 81610

a naturally heated outdoor pool,
Glenwood Hot Springs is the
largest of its kind

White River National Forest
Old Federal Building
P.O. Box 948
Glenwood Springs, CO 81601
(303) 954-2521

for information on camping and
recreation in the area

Grand Junction

Chamber of Commerce
360 Grand Avenue
Grand Junction, CO 81501
(303) 242-3214

Colorado National Monument
Fruita, CO 81521
(303) 858-3617

4 miles west of Grand Junction
off CO 340, a 22-mile circular
drive along canyon rims. Rim
Rock Drive is accessible from
either Fruita or Grand Junction

Grand Valley to Lake Powell

Westwater Canyon
Bureau of Land Management
P.O. Box M
Sand Flats Road
Moab, UT 84532
(801) 259-8193

easy floating from Fruita to
Westwater Ranger Station. Below
that, experts only

Arches and Canyonlands
   National Parks
446 S. Main Street
Moab, UT 84532
(801) 259-7164

From Moab, Arches is 5 miles
west on US 191; Canyonlands is
20 miles SW. Spring/fall are
ideal seasons. Float trips, jeep
trails, mountain biking, camping

Canyonlands Field Institute					seminars, trips for all ages
Box 68
Moab, UT 84532
(801) 259-7750

Ken Sleight Books
550 N. Main
P.O. Box 1270
Moab, UT 84532
(801) 259-8575

Ken Sleight Pack Trips					guided tours for small groups;
  and Trail Rides					1–6 hours
(801) 259-5505

Tex's River Expeditions
P.O. Box 67
Moab, UT 84532
(801) 259-5101

Moab Travel Council
805 N. Main
Moab, UT 84532
(801) 259-8825

Glen Canyon National					houseboating mecca; Rainbow
  Recreation Area					Bridge, tours of dam
P.O. Box 1507
Page, AZ 86040
(602) 645-2471

San Juan Marina					Navajo-run marina on Lake
356 S. Main					Powell, reached from Monument
Blanding, UT 84511					Valley

Monument Valley

Goulding's Lodge   scenic backway to Lake Powell
Monument Valley, UT 84536

Lee's Ferry to Overton

Grand Canyon National Park   easy floats are available from
P.O. Box 129   Glen Canyon Dam to Lee's Ferry.
Grand Canyon, AZ 86023   Below, there's no turning back.
(602) 638-2411   List of raft companies available
                                     from park

Kaibab National Forest   quiet camping on Grand
800 S. 6th Street   Canyon's edge
Williams, AZ 86046
(602) 635-2681

Lake Mead to the Gulf of California

Lake Mead National   houseboating, wind-surfing,
   Recreation Area   sailing, fishing
601 Nevada Highway
Boulder City, NV 89005
(702) 293-4041

Hoover Dam   tours
Bureau of Reclamation
Boulder City, NV 89005
(702) 293-8367

Laughlin, Nevada Chamber   gambling
   of Commerce
P.O. Box 2280
Laughlin, NV 89046
(702) 298-2214

Lake Havasu State Park
(602) 855-7851

Havasu National Wildlife Refuge
1406 Bailey Avenue
Box A
Needles, CA 92363
(619) 326-3853

London Bridge Resort
1477 Queen's Bay Road
Lake Havasu City, AZ 86403
(602) 855-0888

Bureau of Land Management
P.O. Box 5680
Yuma, AZ 85364
(602) 726-6300

Imperial National Wildlife   bird watching
   Refuge
P.O. Box 2217
Martinez Lake, AZ 85364
(602) 783-3400